THE
CAREGIVER'S
GAME

UNRAVELING FINANCIAL DECEIT IN THE
SHADOWS OF DEMENTIA

CHARLES E. WALLACE JR.

Book Cover by Khurram Shahbaz (99designs/Designblunt)

First edition 2025

ISBN: 979-8-9933144-1-9 (paperback)

ISBN: 979-8-9933144-0-2 (ebook)

To my mother, my dad, and my siblings.

Author's Note

I started writing *The Caregiver's Game: Unraveling Financial Deceit in the Shadows of Dementia* in 2024 as a way to process the unspeakable deception my mother and family experienced at the hands of an unscrupulous caretaker who stole hundreds of thousands of dollars from her and little by little took over her decision-making abilities, gaining control of her estate and medical care behind our backs.

In writing this memoir, I've relied on my personal memories and experiences as well as an extensive list of events that occurred between 2017 and 2024. To the best of my ability, I've worked hard to ensure this memoir is a fair and honest portrayal of the events. The memoir is also a recounting of my often difficult relationship with my mother, a narcissistic and serial bride, which made helping her help herself incredibly difficult over the course of her battle with dementia. However, the memory is fallible and my perspective might conflict with others' memories mentioned in this memoir. The stories I retell in this memoir are mine and mine alone. To protect the privacy of certain individuals, some names and other distinguishing characteristics have been changed. The dialogue in the book captures the essence of the story but is not always a word-for-word account.

As of the writing of this book, I'm still actively pursuing answers and trying to piece together the real story of what happened to my mother, who passed away in March 2022. I believe my mother was the victim of a crime syndicate that continues to deceive other unsuspecting families. I intend for this memoir to be a cautionary tale to family members of loved ones who've been diagnosed with dementia and how to protect them from predators, so often disguised as caregivers, who want nothing more than to prey on individuals for financial gain. Through my story, I hope to offer some measure of understanding and support to other family members who've been affected by such callousness and help them find some peace and a sense of justice.

—·—

MARCH 2022

"That's it?"

I stood in the doorway of a dimly lit storage facility, slack-jawed. My wife, Rachel, and my youngest daughter, Kelsey, stood beside me, equally shocked. Larry, my mother's trusted CPA and power of attorney for nearly thirty years, who had accompanied us, didn't say anything.

"Seriously, that's *it*?" I asked again.

"Yes," he replied.

"Where's the rest? The boxes of family heirlooms, photo albums, the furniture from the condo?"

"She told me no one wanted to pay to move the furniture. She gave everything away," he said, in his thick, indifferent east Texas drawl.

"And by 'she,' you mean my mother?"

"Yes, of course."

"And you didn't question it? She had dementia, Larry."

Larry offered nothing more than a shrug. I didn't know what to say. How could three generations of family history from my mother's 2,300-square-foot condo be completely gone?

Of course, I knew the answer. The blame fell solely on Esmarelda, the caregiver my mother had hired four years earlier. I knew she had taken it all. I just didn't have enough evidence to prove it. Only gut suspicions.

"You spoke with Wendy when Mother moved to her assisted living apartment. You didn't think to ask my sister what to do with our mother's things? I can't believe this!"

"Listen, your mother said no one wanted to pay to have the furniture delivered here or to her new place. She gave most of it away to charity." He seemed satisfied with his answer.

I wasn't.

In early 2021, my sister Wendy told me she wanted to keep some furniture and to put them in storage for the time being. Clearly, that request was ignored. No one called us to ask about the so-called charitable donations. No one emailed. Not my mother, not Larry, and certainly not Esmarelda. Now all those pieces were gone.

"Your mother had been spending a lot of money on storage for things she wasn't using. I encouraged her to empty it," Larry tried to explain, which to me was nothing more than a flimsy, half-hearted attempt to justify his lack of oversight. Some power of attorney he was. I know if he'd told Wendy or me what had been being discussed, we'd still have our family's cherished items. Wendy would've told him to leave the storage unit alone. We'd figure it out together as a family.

I took in what little was left in the unit: a few substantial, ornate mirrors and some framed prints saved by grandmother's uncles during the Great Depression. They'd run an art gallery in New Orleans, and when business went south, they'd rolled the pictures up, stored them in a secret location, hiding them from the bank. Years later, my grandmother inherited the framed prints and hung them in her home. Eventually, they were passed on to my mother. The storage unit also contained a child's wooden rocking chair some fifty-plus years old that my grandmother owned when we were young. The rocking chair, like much of the heirlooms passed down from generation to generation on my mother's side, weren't mass-produced pieces. You couldn't replace them with a Target run. They were special. They meant something.

The emptied storage unit confirmed what I'd feared had been happening for the last few years of my mother's life. Esmarelda had slowly been erasing my mother from existence and stealing her life.

Over eighty years of my maternal family's history was gone. Photographs of my great grandmother, my grandmother and grandfather, my mother, my sister and brother, and of my youth—gone.

"I have the receipts Esmarelda sent me. I can send them to you," Larry seemed to offer as part proof, part consolation.

Receipts meant nothing. What meant something was the box of 8mm film I'd found in Mother's condo in 2018. I had planned to have those old movies digitized once the will was settled. There were images of my siblings and I taking our first steps, learning how to roller skate with pillows belted to our backsides, and playing with our first puppy.

"Yes," I finally said, "please do while I'm here this week."

I turned to my wife, Rachel. She was despondent, shocked, and angry. "I can't believe the photos are gone, especially the ones of your mother when she was young. She *never* would have agreed to that!"

Dementia had taken a lot from my mother, but it hadn't taken her vanity or her narcissism. Mother prided herself on always being put together, no matter her age or mental state. She never left the house without her makeup, lipstick, and jewelry on. She held herself like a camera was always in the room, poised and ready for a close-up much like the character Norma Desmond in the 1950 movie *Sunset Boulevard*, always standing, never seated. What dementia had stolen from my mother was her wariness of others. As the disease progressed, she trusted those she shouldn't and dismissed her family's concerns.

She'd made friends with a woman who provided caretaking services across the hallway from her at her apartment complex. Esmarelda. A woman who sneaked her bagels, gained her trust, faked a friendship, and ultimately, took everything from her. Although I had my suspicions about Esmarelda early on, I put them aside.

Mother lived in Dallas. My family lived in the St. Louis Metro area. My siblings were on the West Coast, Wendy in Washington and Eric in California. I wanted to believe this woman's intentions were pure. I wanted to believe she cared for my mother. Standing in the doorway of the near-empty storage unit, I realized just how wrong I'd been—and what I knew then was nothing compared to what I would learn as the mystery unraveled.

PART ONE

MOTHER

1

JOELL

Did I love my mother? Of course I did, but our relationship was complicated. I suppose most parent/child relationships can be described that way—or not—but I think it's safe to assume that every parent/child relationship has its struggles. First in the early formative years when children test the limits and then the teenage years when the limits get tested further. Even the most loving relationships can feel strained at times, but things always seemed slightly different with Mother.

Mother. Sounds kind of like we lived in our version of Alfred Hitchcock's classic movie, *Psycho*. I promise that wasn't the case. We called her Mother because Mom and Pop were reserved for her parents, my maternal grandparents. But I admit, the moniker seems rather cold, but it's rather fitting.

Joell Fleming was not a warm person. Born in 1939 to Dorothy Jo Fisher and Nathan Fink, she grew up to be a harsh critic, seeming to take a certain sort of pleasure in reminding you of your faults, recalling embarrassing details of things you'd rather forget. If I showed you photos of her throughout her life, you'd probably argue with me. How could someone who looked so pleasant be so sharp-tongued? Don't let photos fool you. Mother's kindness—her love——was surface level at best.

Maybe that's why she went through five husbands. My siblings joked that Mother was a serial marriage partner—a cheater, too, we suspected.

Mother cared about status. She wanted the world to view her a certain way, like a Southern socialite. It was how she grew up. Mother was "old" money. And old money had a certain way of doing things like having portraits painted of themselves. Sometime in the 1950s, my grandmother had a portrait of Mother commissioned. Mother had been in her late teens, and in the portrait, she wore a strapless off-white gown with a full tiered skirt and a delicate bracelet on her left wrist. Her dark hair, in a 1950's curled style just above her shoulders, stood out against her milky, youthful skin. Throughout Mother's life, that portrait hung in a spot in any place she lived where it was the first thing you saw when you entered a room. Her attachment to that portrait was undeniably deep. The portrait painted Mother how she saw herself and how she wanted others to see her, even if it wasn't an accurate depiction of who she really was at her core.

Perhaps Mother's parenting style was a sign of her generation and class, but that didn't change the fact that she was a hard mother to have. She didn't show love the way I'd seen my friends' parents show it. She didn't really show interest in my hobbies or my ideas about life.

I played many organized sports throughout my boyhood and teenage years. I loved kicking the soccer ball and playing basketball. Playing sports made me happy. You'd think my mother would've been happy too, but I can count on one hand how many times she showed up to a game. She was more interested in her love life. At that time of my life, she went through three husbands.

The way Mother showed "love" was by buying me and my siblings things. Of course, what she bought came with conditions. Everything Mother did was controlled, never extravagant, but enough to convince us (and others) we were loved.

I remember the time she bought me a new bike when I was about ten years old because my old one wore out from riding it so much. I loved riding my bike all over town. It was my ticket to freedom. I especially enjoyed riding it to my grandmother's house, where she made me food we didn't get at home.

At home, Mother had strict food rules in the house. Everything we ate had to have very little sugar, which meant no non-diet sodas, sugary cereals, or other sweets. I believe her strictness had little to do with ensuring we ate healthy and much more to do with keeping us from becoming fat.

Mother put a great deal of emphasis on her appearance and kept herself trim, slender. Dare I say skinny enough to appear frail at times? She wanted her children to stay skinny too, especially my sister. She body-shamed her often, along with her daughter, and eventually, she did the same to my daughters. My mother always had someone in her crosshairs.

She made us meals at home, but the meals my grandmother made for us were different. It's why I loved to eat at her house. My favorite meal she made was French toast with white bread. Gosh, it was like dessert for breakfast. We didn't get it at home because it had too much sugar. She also made us bologna sandwiches on white bread. They were so good.

Mother didn't like us eating at Grandmother's as much as we did. As I got older, I heard my mother complaining to my grandmother that it took several days to get us back on track after eating at her house.

I could write an entire book just on the trauma and dysfunction I lived through growing up, but that's not what this book is about. This book is about the last years of my mother's life that were stolen.

Mother had dementia, a horrific disease that stripped away her essence. Joell Fleming had never been a trusting person. She didn't see the good in people. She wasn't a charitable person unless it benefited her in some way. She sought attention and accolades, not meaningful relationships. When I began to see Mother through the lens of adulthood, I realized she didn't really have friends. She had collections of people who could help her get what she wanted: jobs, relationships, social status. Often, when her marriages ended, her exes got "custody" of the friends. Mother was someone who was only ever looking out for herself. She used people, until dementia turned the tables and someone used her.

A woman named Esmarelda Gomez put herself in my mother's path, "befriending" her for what I believe was for one purpose: financial gain. I don't want to talk badly about Mother in her absence. As much as she kept an emotional distance from me most of my life, I did love her. She was my mother and cared for me to the best of her abilities, which were often wanting and could even border on emotional abuse at times.

However, I never wanted anything bad to happen to her. I wanted her to live a peaceful life during her last chapter. I wanted to have a closer relationship with her as I grew older, but I lived several states away from her. She lived in Texas. I lived in Illinois. The distance and, subsequently, her dementia formed a gap that left Mother vulnerable to a con woman.

Esmarelda took advantage of my mother's failing mind. She took advantage of the physical distance between my mother and her children. She saw my mother as a lottery ticket, stealing from her right under her nose and robbing myself and my siblings of not only our inheritance, but also the last couple years of Mother's life when she manipulated her into stonewalling us.

I never got the chance to have a day in court with Esmarelda or her co-conspirators in what I believe is a crime syndicate—albeit small potatoes compared to some—that targets elderly individuals for financial gain. That upsets me, but what upsets me most is that Mother died believing Esmarelda was her friend, someone who had her best interests at heart and wouldn't take advantage of her.

I don't want that to happen to someone else.

2

— · —

CHANGES

D ementia is hard. It's duplicitous, mischievous, and unpredictable. It's a liar. It's a disease that infiltrates the person's mind and body slowly, at first, until the person becomes nothing more than a shell of their former self.

Dementia doesn't stop with the person it has pervaded. It's hell-bent on tricking the person's friends and family too. It holds back just enough in the beginning to make you doubt yourself about just how bad your loved one's cognitive abilities have declined. You second-guess yourself constantly, dismissing unusual behaviors as quirks. Mother's just being Mother. Dad's just being Dad. Even when your suspicions grow, you continue to allow the disease to deceive you for a myriad of reasons, with denial often being the number one reason because you know dementia changes everything, and, let's be honest, you're not ready for that either. But whether you're ready or not, dementia doesn't care.

My sister, Wendy, first noticed the problem in early June of 2017. "Mother's having trouble recognizing numbers," she told me.

"What do you mean?" I asked.

"Writing them, reciting them, it's becoming harder for her to do. It's taking her twice as long as normal."

What's normal? In June of 2017, Mother was seventy-eight years old, not old-old but certainly not young. I don't remember being overly concerned. After all, even as a *younger* man in my fifties, I forgot the occasional phone number, account number, or even a birthday. Technology has programmed us to remember less and rely on phones and calendar apps to keep track of these things.

My issue with Mother wasn't her number recognition. I had concerns about her hearing. She had trouble talking on the phone if she couldn't use the speaker on a phone. Any time I visited her, the television's volume was deafening.

You never got far discussing anything with Mother she didn't want to hear. If the matter at hand didn't pertain to something that interested her, she didn't care.

"Mother, have you considered getting hearing aids?" I asked her one day when I called to catch up and see how she'd been doing.

She dismissed me. Joell Fleming would never be caught dead with hearing aids. You can't stop aging, but you can make the process easier. Mother wanted nothing to do with ease. Her vanity was legendary—something my siblings and I found funny and exhausting. Mother prided herself on always being put together, a full face of makeup with her couldn't-live-without lipstick. Her jewelry was always spot-on. No matter the task or the event, you could count on Joell Fleming looking flawless. A hearing aid would have ruined the look.

When she acted dismissive, I didn't push much. The years leading up to the summer of 2017, we didn't talk often. The disinterest she had in my life as a child continued into adulthood. She was only slightly interested in what I had to say, not showing much interest in my life or that of her grandkids. We'd talk thirty to sixty minutes at a time, once every few weeks, mostly about superficial stuff. However, as the summer

14

progressed, things changed one day in late July when she called to tell me she had Lyme disease.

"My doctor says it's the reason I'm having memory problems. Dan's too." Dan was my Mother's fifth husband, my fourth stepfather. Mother's doctor had suggested Dan also get tested for Lyme disease.

Dan had been married multiple times as well. At one point, he was married to a "Golden Girl" for a short time. They were still friends and would talk randomly. I knew this because my mother loved to announce when the famous actress had called. Dan was pretty independent and easygoing. At times, he would go away for the weekend to drive in races at tracks in the region. That was his "sanctuary" from my mother.

I'd also been pretty dismissive of the concerns Wendy had because I believed the problems Mother exhibited were nothing more than the normal results of getting older. Apparently, though, Mother had been concerned too. She just hadn't said anything. I didn't know much, if anything, about dementia at that time, but Lyme disease causing her memory problems? How was that possible, and was Lyme disease even probable? Mother and Dan didn't live anywhere near a wooded area. They lived their lives surrounded by cement 24/7 in their Dallas condo.

"You don't have to live by the woods to get Lyme disease," Mother told me. Her doctor had told her she could get it from mosquito bites or from body fluid transfers. "He's put Dan and I on antibiotics. It's a thirteen-month treatment."

I'm no doctor, but what she was telling me seemed preposterous. Thirteen months taking an antibiotic for Lyme disease? And then the situation turned even stranger.

"The antibiotic can't be ordered from my pharmacy though. It can only be ordered from a town in New Zealand. Oh, and we have to take these special mail-order vitamins."

It all sounded bizarre and incredibly scammy. Was this doctor even a real doctor?

"What does Dan think?" I asked.

Mother quieted. I asked her again. She told me he wasn't on board with the diagnosis or treatment, but he agreed to start the regimen. Dan used to go along sometimes just to keep the peace.

Dementia wasn't something at the forefront of our minds with Mother, but it had become clear she had concerns about her memory and she didn't want to accept it could be a neurological issue. Her doctor gave her a more acceptable diagnosis, and she decided to run with it. Yet if Mother had dementia (and at that point, I wasn't sure she did), we had to intervene sooner rather than later. Rachel, like me, was concerned that delaying a proper diagnosis and medical treatment could cause the disease to progress faster.

"Do you believe this, Rachel?" I asked my wife after my conversation with Mother. She was a pharmacist. Certainly she'd know if such a treatment made sense.

"Not for a second."

Our concerns about the treatment her so-called doctor had prescribed for her and Dan weren't unfounded. Within a few weeks after beginning the regimen, Dan began experiencing increased memory issues. His behavior had become erratic too. A couple times, Mother called expressing her concerns. Dan was getting lost driving to places he had been driving to for years. Dan was eight years older than Mother, and aside from hearing issues, I had no idea he struggled with memory issues until he and Mother began the bogus Lyme disease treatment. At one point, she told me she was afraid he might kill her. Soon after the last of those calls, in August of 2017, we learned his kids moved him to Austin, where he entered an assisted living facility for memory issues. The abrupt move left Mother unsettled.

For the first time in decades, Mother found herself living alone. She didn't take to the change very well. She seemed depressed. I didn't know what to do. I lived six hundred miles away, but I was still the closest relative. I called her more often over the next few weeks. She sounded different, not like her usual self, but I chalked it up to her living alone. She'd been married five times, but in between marriages, she was never really alone. There'd always been kids around to fill the silence.

Mother must have started to get concerned too because in early September, she contacted her physician to discuss her mood changes. He prescribed medication, but her lifestyle had irrevocably changed. She had not driven in over a year and was experiencing increasing difficulty with her hands. Listening to Mother speak of her challenges, I knew I had to come see her. I couldn't ignore the situation any longer. Also, I wanted to get to the bottom of the Lyme disease nonsense and figure out once and for all what we were dealing with. I told her I'd see her at the end of the month.

3

— · —

VITAMINS

SEPTEMBER 2017

I arrived at Mother's condo one late-September afternoon. She lived in a high-rise building called the Athena. The north Dallas building had been constructed in the late 1960s and included twenty-one floors and several penthouses. The condo had originally been my grandmother's, but after she passed away in 1995, my mother sold her house and moved into the condo, executing an elaborate renovation of the master suite, the guest bedroom, and the main living space.

Mother never did anything halfway or cheap. The renovation involved enclosing the patio spaces to create a larger master suite, installing hardwood flooring, and removing a hallway between two of the bedrooms to create a ginormous master bath and walk-in closet. We joked that shopping was Mother's job. She needed a warehouse for her designer bags, shoes, and outfits. She couldn't have that, so she built the largest closet she could in the given space.

When Mother opened the door, she was wearing a nightgown and looked thinner than I'd ever seen her before—and that was saying something. Mother was always a thin woman, reminding me of the slim Parisian models of the past before France banned extremely thin models.

Mother's excessive thinness and lack of proper daytime dress wasn't normal.

I hugged her bony frame, chatted with her briefly, then walked to the condo's extra bedroom to put my bags down. I returned to the kitchen, opened the refrigerator to get something to drink, and discovered a fridge filled less than twenty percent. Mother clearly wasn't taking care of herself, and it left me teeming with worry. Did she need more help than I realized? I decided to wait until the morning to find out more about how she was managing alone.

That morning, at breakfast, I made us eggs and toast. While we sat together at the kitchen bar to eat, I asked her how she'd been eating.

"So, Mother, what do you normally eat for breakfast?"

"Oh, it depends. I'll make a small bowl of oatmeal and have some fruit. Or maybe an egg with some coffee," she said proudly.

"I think you may not be eating enough," I suggested.

"Oh, I'm good. I weigh about ninety-five pounds."

Ninety-five pounds? I didn't like that number. But how do you tell your mother you think she's starving herself, intentionally or not? It's a fine line adult children and their parents walk. You don't want to parent the parent unnecessarily, but you don't want to ignore obvious problems either.

"I think that sounds a little light. Here, let's grab a calorie counter app, and we can see what you might need to eat for breakfast." A quick search in the app store on my phone provided me with a useful calorie tracking app.

"What did you have to eat yesterday?"

She walked me through what she could recall eating at each meal the previous day. Immediately, I recognized the issue.

"Do you know you are eating less than a thousand calories a day? That is way too low."

"But I don't feel like I'm eating too little," she responded.

"Is there anything else you are eating or taking?"

"Yes, I have those vitamins that are supposed to help my memory from my doctor."

"Can I see them?"

"Sure. They're over there on the counter by the coffee machine."

I walked to the counter and picked up three so-called vitamin containers, one by one, turning them over in my hand and reading every word on the label. The containers looked like nothing I'd seen before. I took pictures with my phone.

"Mother, I'm going to my bedroom for a bit. Will you be okay?"

She barely acknowledged me, instead picking at her breakfast, eating very little.

In my bedroom, I pulled out my laptop and searched online for the company listed on the containers. The search led me to a website with very little information. The website consisted of two pages: one that listed their vitamins and another for providers. The providers' page was nothing more than an affiliate page, letting providers know how to sign up to receive a commission for each recommendation that resulted in a sale.

On the vitamin information page, a photo of each vitamin container was displayed along with a little information about the formula, what it was for, and the footnotes for the research done to support the vitamin's benefits. I read through the PDFs referenced in the footnotes looking for anything that might support Mother's doctor putting her on this regimen for her memory issues. At the very end of one of the documents I read, I found a sentence claiming the vitamin might help with memory improvement. The vitamins were not approved by the Food and Drug Administration (FDA). They were not part of a treatment plan prescribed to memory-impaired patients by their physicians only after comprehensive studies had been done on the effectiveness of the drug. In my opinion, these vitamins were nothing more than placebos given to unsuspecting patients by their doctors for one purpose only—to receive financial compensation.

What a waste of time! If Mother was exhibiting signs of dementia, she needed a neurologist, not a doctor worried about padding his pockets with money from commission-based product sales. She needed help now, not twelve months down the road when she discovered firsthand that the diagnosis and the treatment were a crock.

I scrolled through some doctor review sites, looking for any information I could find about the doctor that could strengthen my case to Mother. After a few dead ends, I found an entry on a site from an irate woman written just a year earlier about Mother's doctor. The woman wrote that her mother had memory issues and the doctor told her the same thing he'd told Mother, that it was Lyme disease. The woman knew that didn't make sense. She immediately sensed that this doctor was selling Lyme disease as a diagnosis for his own financial gain. She pulled her mother from the doctor's practice and found a neurologist.

But would Mother believe me when I showed her this review? She'd always been set in her opinions and quick to dismiss anyone who disagreed with her. I also knew that if Mother's concerns about her memory were more than she led on, that turning a deaf ear to my protestations about the vitamins and the quack doctor might be rooted in something more powerful than pride. It might be rooted in fear. Accepting a Lyme disease diagnosis with a treatment plan was much easier than accepting a dementia diagnosis with a tragic outcome.

I didn't know how to help her. I wanted to flush those damn vitamins down the toilet and drag her to a neurologist, but I knew I couldn't do any of that. Mother might have been struggling with recalling numbers and having some hearing problems. She was definitely underweight and not acting like herself, but none of those things took away her power to make decisions for herself. Even though I started to suspect something more was going on with her neurologically, I couldn't do anything about it, and I couldn't stay with her indefinitely. Eventually, I had to go back home. I also couldn't check on her every weekend. We lived too far apart. So what could I do something about?

I mulled over the situation all night, getting very little sleep, but by breakfast the next morning, I had an idea.

"Mother, have you ever thought of hiring someone to cook for you?"

I couldn't make Mother stop taking her vitamins or see a neurologist, but if she didn't start eating better, she would waste away to nothing. Her nutrition needed attention, and having someone come in and cook meals for her might help.

Mother gave me a quizzical look and said, "I haven't."

"You could afford it."

"Who would I ask? Do you know someone?"

I didn't but said, "I'm sure other people in the building pay for help like that. Maybe you could ask some people. See if you can get some referrals?"

"Hmm, yes, that might be a good idea. I'm sure I could ask around."

"Good, good," I said, feeling relieved and slightly victorious. I might've solved her most immediate problem—for now. Bringing someone in to cook for her would keep her physically healthy.

Never did I ever imagine that one tiny suggestion would turn my Mother's life completely upside down and turn our lives into a nightmarish hell over the next five years.

4

A NEW FRIEND

MARCH 2018

Since visiting my mother at her condo at the end of September the previous year, things seemed to level out. I still called to check in on her from time to time. I still tried to dissuade her from participating in the bogus Lyme disease protocol. Yet, Mother was Mother. She was going to do what she wanted to do, and no one could tell her any different; her stubbornness had only gotten worse with age.

Her wariness of people had also been a constant trait throughout her life. Mother kept her collection of people at a distance because, quite frankly, she thought she was better than everyone. It was only when she needed something that she'd bring someone into her fold—and not usually for long. So when Wendy called me in February 2018 and told me Mother had a new friend she recently met, I was flabbergasted.

"What the hell does that mean?" I asked. Never had I known my mother to call someone a friend she had just met. I would learn much later that this is a common ploy of abusive caregivers to have their victim identify them as a "friend."

"I don't know. She told me she has a new friend. The caregiver of a woman who lives next door to her. She said the neighbor isn't eating all her food, so she should have it," Wendy explained further. "She says she's been sneaking her bagels."

"I wonder if it's the woman she hired to make meals for her now?" Mother had mentioned she hired someone to help her cook meals. Over the last several months, Mother's memory issues had begun to worsen. I wondered if she forgot she'd hired someone to help with meals, believing instead the woman to be a cohort.

"Kelsey's spring break is in a couple of weeks. It's been a while since she's seen her grammy. I think we'll take a trip to Dallas to see what Mother's up to," I told Wendy. "I'll let you know what I find out."

I wasn't sure how much information my mother would give me about her new friend. I expected her to stay quite mum on the subject, but that wasn't the case at all. It wasn't long after Kelsey and I arrived at her place that she started gushing about this woman named Esmarelda, her unbridled excitement reminiscent of a middle-school girl going on and on about her crush.

"Esmarelda made us lunch and a couple of dinners too. They're in the fridge. Now we don't have to go out so much," Mother said excitedly.

"Oh, okay, great," I replied less enthusiastically than Mother about the prospect of staying in for meals. When we visited Mother, we wanted to go out. Eating at local restaurants and getting out of the condo was our reward for coming to town.

Although I still planned to go out for some meals while we were in town, I thought it wouldn't hurt to see what was in the refrigerator. I don't know what I expected, but I certainly didn't expect to open the refrigerator door and see enough food to feed a family of six for a week, at least. Or a refrigerator that looked like a cooler at a warehouse club like Sam's or Costco. Even when my family of four hosted Christmas dinner, we'd never had a refrigerator jam-packed with the amount of food in Mother's.

Kelsey came up behind me, peered over my shoulder, and said, "Wow."

What else could you say?

Mother had walked into the kitchen and found us staring, jaws open, at the refrigerator's contents. "Esmarelda gave us extra food because she won't be around this weekend," she explained. "She's actually bringing lunch over in a little bit, so you can meet her."

About an hour later, Esmarelda Gomez arrived, letting herself in and carrying a couple of paper bags containing more food.

"Hi," she said, slightly out of breath from carrying the groceries. She put the groceries down, ran her hands through her reddish-brown hair, and reached out to take my hand as I introduced myself.

"Nice to meet you. Your mom said you really like Tex-Mex, so I brought enchiladas, rice and beans, and some soup for lunch."

I couldn't quite land on Esmarelda's age, but I placed her in her mid-sixties, slightly older than I expected. She was slim, about five feet five inches, and wore scrubs. She seemed very comfortable in Mother's home. She seemed nice enough, but as she chatted away, I couldn't help but get the feeling I was meeting the female version of Eddie Haskell, the charming yet untrustworthy neighbor on the 1950s television show *Leave It to Beaver*.

Esmarelda began preparing our lunch, which did look delicious, but I couldn't stop thinking about all the food in the refrigerator and the food currently being prepared. So much food! Who was going to eat all that food? And, more importantly, who was paying for it all?

"Why is there so much food in the refrigerator?" I asked Esmarelda. "It seems like a lot for one person."

"Oh, well you know your mom. She doesn't like to eat the same thing often. So, I make extra food."

Hmm. That little tidbit of information was new to me. I remembered Mother talking about going days only eating from the Whole Foods' salad bar with Dan. She was a woman who could make a seven-ounce beer last for days. Her entire life, she ate the same thing and never a lot because she didn't want to feel too full.

Lunch hit the spot, and I could see why Mother enjoyed Esmarelda's cooking, but still a question tugged at me.

"Are you giving my mother receipts from the grocery store for all these food purchases?"

If I surprised Esmarelda with my questions, she didn't show it.

"No," she said matter-of-factly. "I tell her what I paid, and she reimburses me."

Her answer didn't please me one bit. It left too much wiggle room for dishonesty. Like Mother, I could be a bit untrusting too.

"I think it would be a good idea to start giving Mother the receipts, or even myself. Is that something we can start doing from here on out?"

The smile she wore throughout lunch, the jovial personality, disappeared. "Well, I work for your mom, as you know. If she wants me to give her receipts, she will need to ask for them."

Esmarelda's tone didn't please me one bit. I turned to Mother, who by then sat demurely at the kitchen bar. I knew she had heard our conversation, but she didn't say a word to Esmarelda about needing receipts. Her lack of response frustrated me because I knew if Mother were anywhere close to her normal self, she wouldn't have offered to reimburse for anything without a receipt. Heck, several years back, she'd taken photos of her condo when she'd had contractors in and out performing renovations. "For insurance purposes," she had told me. "In case something goes missing."

Her not asking Esmarelda to see receipts before reimbursing her went against Mother's distrustful nature, and it further cemented what I'd been worried about for some time since the whole Lyme disease treatment mess: Mother couldn't live alone, and I didn't have a good solution.

I decided to drop the receipt request, vowing to myself to bring it up at a later time with Mother when we were alone. After lunch, Esmarelda left. I wouldn't see her again for six months, but that didn't mean she disappeared. Quite the opposite. She continued to insert herself into Mother's life in ways I'd never imagined.

5

LOST

MARCH 2018

Touring McMansions in overpriced neighborhoods is something my family and I do for fun. It's interesting to see different layouts, to pick apart the homeowner's head-scratching choices, while equally oohing and aahing over ornate fixtures and luxury touches. While we were visiting with Mother over spring break, my daughter discovered an open house for a ginormous ten-million-dollar spec home not far from my mother's place. I thought it would be fun to take her to the house, do something different, and get out of the condo.

After lunch, we drove to the house. Already, numerous cars were parked up and down the street. Fortunately, I found a space near the house's front entrance and hightailed it into the empty space before another vehicle could swoop in and take it. Parking in front of the house made it easier to get Mother inside without having to walk a long distance, and let me tell you this...she moved slowly.

Mother's mobility had declined considerably between my visit in September 2017 and now. Simple things you and I take for granted, like taking our seat belts off and stepping out of the car, were becoming increasingly difficult for Mother. Once I helped her out of the car, she held onto my arm and shuffled her feet while walking. It took us quite a bit of time to make it up the long circular driveway. Maybe this is a mistake, I thought. Yet I knew Mother liked the lifestyles of the rich and famous, believing herself to be in the upper echelon of society too, even if her wealth wasn't close to on par with individuals who could purchase a ten-million-dollar home. As we entered the house's front entry, with its twenty-foot ceilings, marble flooring, and stunning chandelier, I spied a smile creep across my mother's face. This will be fine, I told myself. Just fine.

I saw a table positioned against one of the walls in the entry with a stack of Realtor sheets resting on it. I walked over to the table, plucked a sheet from the stack, then noticed a curved staircase leading to the second floor.

"Let's go this way," I suggested, motioning toward the staircase.

My daughter gave me an inquiring look. How is Grammy getting up those stairs? I surveyed the area and saw an elevator. Of course, a ten-million-dollar house would have an elevator, and what a perfect solution.

"Mother," I said, taking her arm and leading her to the elevator, "you take the elevator, and Kelsey and I will take the stairs. We'll meet you on the second floor."

Mother nodded. This will work out perfectly, I thought. A great plan. But what do they say about the best-laid plans?

Kelsey and I made it to the second floor in no time at all. Then we waited for the elevator. I hadn't expected a residential elevator to be lightning fast, but it seemed to be taking unnecessarily long to arrive. I walked down the hallway leading away from the elevator to an open walkway and around a corner, not venturing too far from the elevator but still out of sight. I came back around the corner once I realized I would be out of Mother's line of sight when the elevator arrived. As I came around the corner, I saw another woman touring the house standing next to the elevator with her ear to the door. She looked at me, concerned.

"There's someone in there. She can't get out."

It had to be Mother.

"Can she hear you?" I asked.

The woman nodded. "I think so. She says she doesn't know how to make it work."

"It's my mother," I told her.

The woman stepped aside to let me get closer to the door. I knocked on it to get her attention. "Try hitting the button to go to the first floor."

Mother didn't answer, but I heard the elevator's motor start up. I raced down the steps to meet the elevator on the ground level. Relief flooded through me when the elevator doors opened. Thank goodness!

"What happened?" I asked, panting while I caught my breath.

"I don't know. I rode up to the second floor and then it stopped. I tried a couple of the buttons and nothing happened."

She didn't seem frazzled. In fact, she acted nonchalant about the whole thing. Still, while we continued the tour, she did keep going back to the elevator incident, mumbling under her breath here and there about the elevator not working. It seemed to me the elevator worked fine and the kerfuffle was caused by human error. Operating an elevator was definitely something Mother knew how to do, especially living on the fourth floor of the Athena.

But we all have off days, right? That's what I told myself. Maybe Mother was having an off day or the elevator controls looked different. She didn't seem worried. Why was I? And that's the thing about the early stages of dementia. Your brain tells you you're overreacting. Your gut tells you you're not. Your brain can deceive you, but your gut never lies.

I wish I had listened to my gut that day. I wish I had listened to it the day I met Esmarelda. I wished I'd listened to it when I started to doubt other people in my mother's life like Larry, her CPA. But I didn't. And I know I'm not alone. So many loved ones doubt themselves as they watch their parents or other loved ones struggle with cognitive decline, especially when the loved one doesn't acknowledge the decline or recognize a problem. Looking back, I believed Mother's insistence she was fine for far too long. I believed my head over my gut too long, and what a mistake that would turn out to be.

6

—·—

RECORDS

SUMMER 2018

M other had granted Wendy and me medical power of attorney
(MPOA) in December 2017, right around the time she updated her will and named her three children as equal beneficiaries.
Thank goodness she granted us MPOA because she needed someone
helping her figure out her memory issues. Her so-called Lyme disease
treatment would be finished by September, and her memory issues
hadn't improved one bit. If anything, the bogus treatment worsened
her cognitive function because it delayed proper treatment.

Wendy told me she'd spoken to Mother's quack doctor and in-
quired about a neurologist referral.

"He told me he would see what information he had."

I wasn't holding my breath. Why would that doctor be willing
to release his hold on Mother? He'd lose money from her once she
stopped buying those ridiculous supplements.

The next day, I hadn't heard from him, so I called him. His nurse told
me he was busy, but I could set up a phone call for the two of us to chat
the next day. She also asked me to send the MPOA paperwork to them so
they could speak freely with me. I sent those papers over lightning fast,

even though I wasn't sure I'd get a return phone call. To my surprise, though, he actually called the next day when she said he would.

"Thank you for returning my call," I began. "I'm anxious to contact the referrals you have."

"About that," the doctor said. "You see, I'm having some difficulty finding an appropriate referral. Most of my usual referrals have retired."

Of course they had.

"I need to call some of my contacts and see if they have any referrals."

"So, how long will that take?" I asked, not caring one bit about hiding the irritation in my voice.

"It should be a day or so." His noncommittal voice hinted at amusement, as if he was laughing off the situation.

My mother had been losing brain function over the last year because of his con treatment plan, and this man didn't seem to care one bit. He seemed to think it was funny he didn't have a referral.

"It's important to get this referral soon," I insisted. "Mother's treatment plan with you ends in September, and I want something set up with a neurologist sooner rather than later."

"I will get that referral to you as soon as I hear back from my contacts."

"Okay, in the meantime, please send me my mother's medical records. I'd like to review them. Your office has my medical POA on file."

That man infuriated me. I wanted to strangle him through the phone, but I didn't want to burn a bridge just yet. I still needed his help, but really, how in the hell can you have a medical practice that's primarily geriatric patients and not have any neurologist referrals? If you're selling Lyme disease treatment as a cure for memory issues, I guess you don't need neurologist referrals, I reminded myself.

I couldn't wait for Dr. Quack to give me a referral. Mother had waited long enough to get the medical treatment she needed. I opened my laptop and began searching for neurologists in Dallas, reviewing the doctors' ratings and comments made by previous and current patients. I came away from that search with a list of about five neurologists.

It took a few days, but the medical records from Dr. Quack's office showed up. The records were a mess, his comments inconsistent from visit to visit. Some visits he noted with great detail. Other visits had very little detail. What was consistent in the medical records was Mother complaining of still having memory issues despite the treatment. She had mentioned having difficulty holding a pen to sign checks.

The inconsistent note-taking bothered me, but what really floored me were the lab results I found in the records. The Lyme disease testing had been sent to a lab in California. And the results? Inconclusive. Actually, the report I received contained information for Mother and Dan—a huge HIPAA violation since I didn't have any MPOA to receive Dan's information. Mother's results for Lyme disease came back inconclusive, but Dan's? His results came back negative.

I couldn't believe what I was reading. Did Dr. Quack think I wouldn't be able to understand the results in these reports? I can't believe he sent proof to me that he was scamming my mother.

It was time to be done with this doctor and his bogus treatments. It was also evident that Mother had become more and more gullible or, perhaps the right sentiment, more trusting. She was putting her faith in people who didn't necessarily have her best interests at heart.

I began to suspect this during the March 2018 visit when Mother had asked me to help access some documents on her computer. While we were looking at the documents, I noticed a Post-it note on her desk with her broker account login written on it. She'd recently told me she had consolidated all her accounts to the broker's bank, which seemed odd but also convenient. While she was distracted with something on the screen, I grabbed a blank Post-it and wrote the information down. I had no interest in Mother's brokerage accounts before, but something told me I needed to start monitoring her financial situation.

Now, a few months later, I was grateful to have this information. I logged in periodically, mostly to see what she was paying Esmarelda. Mother had written several checks to her. The first few checks seemed pretty normal. Mother had indicated in the memo section on the checks what the money was for, such as salary and food reimbursement. The amounts weren't consistent, so I couldn't get a handle on how much Mother actually paid Esmarelda for her services. The inconsistency of payment amounts bothered me. If Esmarelda had been working specific hours each week, I felt the salary amount (a term I use loosely) shouldn't vary.

Another thing that bothered me was the amount of money Mother paid Esmarelda for food. It seemed astronomical to me because a petite woman like my mother could never eat anywhere near the amount of food Esmarelda bought and prepared. I hadn't pushed the issue the day I met Esmarelda for the first time and she made us lunch at Mother's place, but I'd mentioned it to Wendy a few times since. We both had the same thought: Who else is she feeding?

I couldn't help wondering if she had other clients who she fed and relied on our mother to fund her side business. You might think that's an absurd accusation. Who would do that? Well, at this time, Wendy and I had no idea what was going on. Mother only told us what she wanted, and Esmarelda kept us at a distance. After she told me she worked for Mother and made it clear that she only answered to her, it became obvious that I was at Mother's and Esmarelda's mercy. Mother had hired Esmarelda. Not me. Not Wendy. We had no authority to demand anything from her, like receipts.

Being on the periphery of Mother's decisions didn't sit right with me, but I figured as long as I could log into her accounts and check on her

finances when I needed to, I could control the situation. Oh, how wrong
I was!

7

— • —

THE NEUROLOGIST

OCTOBER 2018

T hirteen months after Mother's bogus Lyme disease treatment and subsequent therapies, she finally had her first neurologist's appointment. I had come down to Dallas to attend the appointment with her. One of the hardest parts of living so far from my mother was not being able to attend every doctor's appointment with her. Previously, when she was younger and certainly not showing signs of dementia, the distance didn't seem so great. She had been healthy enough and of sound mind to handle her health and other aspects of life, even if I did not always agree with her choices. Moreover, nearly seven hundred miles apart boded better for our relationship—or lack thereof. I had grown accustomed to the distance. I knew the boundaries of our relationship, but that is the thing about dementia: boundaries change.

Mother's neurology appointment was later in the morning, giving us ample time to prepare without feeling rushed. As we were about to leave, Esmarelda arrived. Surprise! She was going with us.

By then, Esmarelda's duties had expanded since my last visit. She was no longer just cooking for Mother. Her responsibilities had increased to include overnight stays at my mother's request. She'd also allowed Esmarelda to drive her car whenever needed, a change from the previous arrangement, which had limited driving the car to work-related activities.

Was I pleased Esmarelda came with us? Not really. I would have preferred to spend the time alone with Mother, but she seemed to enjoy Esmarelda's company. So, I didn't make a fuss. One of the challenges faced by many adult children of Alzheimer's and dementia patients is getting their parents to relinquish control and allow family involvement in their medical decisions. I had not experienced much pushback from Mother up to that point, but since she relied on and trusted Esmarelda so much (and at that time, I didn't have significant concerns about Esmarelda's involvement), I thought her presence might be soothing for Mother.

Mother's appointment with the neurologist was in a ten-story medical office building across the street from Texas Health Presbyterian Hospital. The neurologist, Dr. Tanja Janaka, claimed to have, at least according to her website bio, "a fascination with the intricacies of the brain that led her to pursue a career in neurology." I had high hopes for this visit.

Upon our arrival, Mother signed some documents with Esmarelda's assistance, and then we were called into an exam room that consisted of a counter, cabinets along the walls, and several chairs off to the side. Mother sat in the exam chair by the window with Esmarelda standing behind her. The three of us waited quietly for Dr. Janaka to meet with us.

We didn't wait long before hearing a slight knock on the door.

"Hello," Dr. Janaka greeted us. Her demeanor was quiet and slightly reserved. She had a calming presence, which I liked. "How is everyone today?"

We briefly introduced ourselves, and then Dr. Janaka began her questioning of Mother.

"So, Joell, tell me. What's going on? How do you feel?"

"Well, sometimes I can't talk as well as I used to."

Dr. Janaka smiled. "That happens to the best of us. Do you mind if I ask your son and caregiver some questions?"

Mother nodded.

"Tell me, Mr. Wallace, what changes have you noticed in your mother?"

"Well, since her husband moved into an assisted living facility in Austin last year, Mother's been living alone. Well, mostly." I gestured toward Esmarelda. "Esmarelda has been helping my mother with some in-home help since this past February. The last few times I've visited Mother, since her husband moved out, I've noticed she's having increasing cognitive difficulties."

"Are you there all the time?" Dr. Janaka asked Esmarelda.

"Mostly. I also have an assistant who provides care for Joell. One of us is there at all times. The cognitive difficulties are why Joell hired me," Esmarelda said, patting Mother's hand and smiling.

I stiffened. There those words were again: *hired me*. Whether it was intentional or not, Esmarelda had made it clear who had the authority to question any decisions: the person who hired her, a woman whose decision and comprehension skills we were here questioning.

"When I started working with Joell on a more round-the-clock basis, I noticed she had trouble keeping up her home. Everything was a mess. It was clear to me she hadn't been eating regularly, and I'm not sure how regularly she took a bath."

Dr. Janaka nodded. "And Joell, you say you don't talk as well as you used to. What do you mean by that?"

Esmarelda answered for her. "Oh, she does quite well speaking with her family on the phone when they call, but in large groups where Joell doesn't know a lot of people, she seems to have trouble remembering names. Sometimes she can't finish a story while telling it."

My experience with Mother on the phone hadn't matched Esmarelda's description at all. I found phone calls were becoming increasingly challenging. Yes, she could talk about general things for a bit, but not hold a conversation for an extended period. Where in the past we'd spend thirty to forty-five minutes on the phone together, now it was more like ten or fifteen minutes.

And what was this about large groups? Where had Esmarelda and Mother been going? As if reading my thoughts, Esmarelda said, "Joell is having some sadness being away from her husband. She misses him. I've encouraged her to get out more, and she's been going to the grocery store with me. She told me she feels like a person again. Isn't that right, Joell? She's even been exercising twice a day for thirty minutes!"

Esmarelda made herself sound like a miracle for Mother—and it rubbed me the wrong way. But why? Did I feel guilty that me or Wendy couldn't be in town for Mother 24/7? Was I projecting those feelings onto Esmarelda? Or was it something else? Was it my intuition trying to get my attention?

Dr. Janaka thanked us for the information and then produced a piece of paper and placed it in front of Mother. "Would you mind drawing something for me?"

She asked her to copy the shapes on the paper. It seemed straightforward and easy, but not for Mother. Watching the way she held the pencil, the slowness with which she drew the shapes, it struck me how difficult such a simple task was for her. She drew them as if she were doing it for the first time. She acted so childlike at that moment. I always knew her as a confident person, never wanting to appear weak or incapable in front of others. A force to be reckoned with, but not then. In fact, every so often, she would look to Esmarelda for assistance or reassurance.

When she finished the assignment, the drawings were tiny and didn't look anywhere near what she was supposed to draw. The doctor went on to ask her some more questions, performing what is called the Mini-Mental State Examination (MMSE). It's an eleven-question exam that's been used since the mid-1970s to assess cognitive function, specifically in five areas: attention and calculation, language, orientation, recall, and registration. Surprisingly, it's a fast and simple test that takes about five or ten minutes to administer.

Questions she asked my mother included things like: What is the year? What season are we in? Can you spell the word "world" backward? She also asked Mother to write a sentence.

The maximum score you can achieve on the MMSE is 30. A score of 23 or less indicates cognitive impairment. Mother scored a 12, indicating moderate dementia. However, the results of the examination wouldn't come to light for us until many months later because my mother didn't share the results with us. She'd been scheduled follow-up appointments with the neurologist and given a referral to a psychiatrist, but she mentioned none of this to Wendy or me. It was only during the summer of 2019 that Wendy, using her MPOA , got that information.

While the MMSE brought to my attention some of Mother's cognitive sluggishness, I still didn't fully understand how dementia worked. I knew we were at the neurologist's office looking for answers as to why Mother seemed more forgetful and to try and mitigate any damage done from the bogus Lyme disease treatment, but I didn't know a lot about dementia. I'd never experienced anyone with dementia. I had this idea that dementia simply meant Mother might forget her kids' names or how old she was. I didn't realize that dementia would steal more than her memory. It would take her motor skills, her reasoning abilities, and it would make her more susceptible to the influences of people who didn't have her best interests at heart. People like Esmarelda.

8

—·—

CHALLENGED

JULY 2019

L ife moved quickly after Mother's first neurologist appointment. I got busy with work, my family's calendar was constantly full, and I didn't really hear much from my mother other than the occasional phone call. I assumed things with her cognitive health had stayed pretty much steady from last October, until Wendy called me about her visit with her the previous month.

"Mother was a mess last month. She couldn't dress herself. I had to cut up her pancake for her. She couldn't even use her fork. She kept picking it up by the wrong end. She even had to have help putting her bra on!"

The helper? My thirteen-year-old niece, Wendy's daughter. God knows the mental scars that may have left.

Hearing her describe Mother's behavior left me feeling unsure how to move forward. We were in new territory. I never thought we'd escape dementia's grasp, but I wasn't prepared for how to battle against it.

"So, what do you think we should do?" I asked.

"Well, for starters, I'm setting up a Google folder to keep track of all her medical documents and records. I spoke with the neurologist at UT Southwestern and asked them to send over Mother's records. I also asked the neurologist to write a letter describing Mother's mental state. I sent

CHARLES E. WALLACE JR.

Moe, Larry, and Curly a letter outlining the signs of dementia and the steps necessary to help Mother best."

Moe had been one of Mother's fiduciaries, in addition to Larry, and Curly was the attorney referred to mother by Moe.

"How did they respond?"

"I called Moe to talk it over, and he kept saying, 'Oh, your momma is fine.' Very dismissive. But, Chip, you know she's not fine. She's a mess, and they're ignoring it. And Larry? Don't even get me started on him. He refuses to act pursuant to the POA. He says Mother isn't drooling on herself, so he doesn't see where he needs to step in. I told him Mother lies and downplays her condition. That's what people with dementia do. I tried to explain her low scores on the MMSE and how, when she took the Montreal Cognitive Assessment (MoCA), she scored zero in executive function, math, and delayed recall. They won't even test her again because of her low score!"

Wendy went on to tell me how she'd implored Larry to act in Mother's best interest and to protect her from possible outside influences. She asked him to complete a full accounting of Mother's finances, to replace her as trustee, obtain a background check on Esmarelda, require her to report to him, and to do an inventory of the valuables in the condo based on the insurance policy that listed those items.

"I said to him, 'Would you have such a light-touch approach if it were your mother who had dementia?' He didn't answer that question. He only repeated that he'd only do what Mother directly told him."

Listening to Wendy's retelling of her conversation with Larry cemented what I'd been beginning to suspect for some time: the people around Mother couldn't be trusted anymore, if they ever could. We'd trusted them because we thought they were looking out for her. Because we lived so far from her and couldn't uproot our lives to live with her in Dallas, and since she wouldn't come live with us, we needed a support system for her. It was beginning to seem like we'd chosen the wrong people.

"And," Wendy continued, "he refuses to consider the neurologist's letter, a medical professional who deals with dementia patients regularly. He actually said to me, 'I don't know what she's basing that information on, but she seems to me to be able to make decisions.'"

That's the thing about dementia patients I'd begun to understand: They're incredible actors—and why wouldn't they be? They don't want people questioning their decisions constantly. They don't want to admit that the mind that served them so well for most of their life is now failing them, and they're desperate to retain some semblance of control in their life.

It was after this phone call with Wendy, when I opened the Google folder with all the information my sister had gathered, that I saw the results from the first neurologist's test for the first time. As you may recall, Mother didn't share these with us, but now that we had invoked the MPOA, we had the information. We'd had the MPOA since 2017, but we never felt it necessary to use it to access Mother's medical records. We relied on Mother to tell us things. In hindsight, it was clear we should have been more inquisitive and less reliant. I also saw the results from two more tests she had done earlier in the year, one in February and the other in early June. Her score remained steady, still placing her in the moderate-dementia category. Her doctors had prescribed some medicine to alleviate some of the symptoms associated with her memory loss as well as the tremors she had in her hands, but I couldn't gauge how much it was helping. The one thing that came across clearly while reading Mother's medical records was disbelief. I couldn't believe Larry and Moe, the people my mother entrusted her finances to, were ignoring her condition. Or was it something much more sinister than that? Were they exploiting her condition and taking advantage of her? I'd heard of things like that happening but never thought it could happen to us.

A couple of weeks later, I received an envelope postmarked from Dallas. I found this odd considering Mother didn't send physical letters, but maybe letter writing was an easier way for her to communicate. I hadn't spoken to her in a couple of weeks since phone calls had become challenging. In the past, we could chat on the phone for thirty or forty minutes with no problems. But that had changed. Mother's hearing had gotten worse, and she needed to use the speaker on her phone. With our conversations happening over the speaker and knowing Esmarelda or one of the other caregivers were nearby, it made it impossible to have a private conversation.

I opened the letter and found a short typed note. At the end of the note, Mother had presumably signed her name. The sloppy signature resembled something a child would write. The note got to the point fairly quickly.

RE: Medical Power of Attorney

Dear Chip,

I just wanted to let you know that I had to change my MPOA and HIPPA release to someone local in case of an emergency.

The new MPOA is Lynda Coumelis and Stephanie Grimes as an alternate.

Even though I am making this change, I wanted to thank you for your commitment to me and to let you know I appreciate you being there for me.

Sincerely,

Mother

I immediately called Wendy.

"Did you get a letter from Mother?" I asked.

"Yeah. What a bunch of junk!"

"I get her wanting local friends as MPOA in case of an emergency, but she didn't have to remove us completely." I used the term "friends" loosely because, as I'd mentioned before, Mother didn't really have friends. She had people in her life who filled her time, like Lynda and Stephanie, who she occasionally went with to Sunday brunch.

Yes, it irritated me that Wendy and I had been seemingly shoved aside, but what I couldn't shake was the feeling it wasn't entirely Mother's idea to remove us as MPOA. It had to be Esmarelda, trying to wall us off from Mother. Still, I believed it wouldn't get too bad with Larry and Moe watching out for her—at least, I thought they were. Lately, though, they'd been keeping us at arm's length too. Any time we tried contacting them, they told us Mother didn't want them giving us any information. We'd known them for decades, and they had started treating us like strangers.

"You know," Wendy said, "I talked to Larry the other day and asked him to work with Mother to file for her long-term care insurance, but he won't. He said she doesn't want to file, so he won't. He'll only do what Mother tells him."

"Did you speak with Moe?" I asked. Moe had been the person who'd sold Mother the insurance policy. A couple weeks earlier, he'd told Wendy he thought Mother would fail a cognitive evaluation.

"Yeah. No help there. He's reversed his opinion. Thinks she's fine and doesn't need to file a claim. Like Larry, he'll only do what Mother tells him."

"I guess they're more concerned about getting paid than actually protecting her best interests, huh?"

"What do you think about doing a background check on Esmarelda?" Wendy asked.

We never had a background check done on Esmarelda because Mother hadn't thought it was necessary. She'd met Esmarelda because she'd been caregiving for one of Mother's neighbors, and she told us the neighbor was picky about people, so she felt a background check wasn't necessary. If her neighbor was fine with her, then she was fine with her.

I no longer felt it was fine. Something was off. We should've done a background check on her from day one.

"I like that idea a lot. How do we get one? I don't want to buy one off the internet."

"I'll check with some contacts I have in Houston and see who they have worked with. But Chip, we need to find out more about this woman. I'm getting a bad feeling about her."

"I agree."

It took Wendy about a week to find someone. We decided to split the cost for a general background check that should take about a week. I hoped it wouldn't cost a fortune, but Wendy was right; we needed to find out more about Esmarelda.

The days seemed to creep by while I waited for the report. I tried to stay busy with work, but even with a full workload, I couldn't keep the anticipation at bay. I was anxious to find out what the background check would reveal.

It took a full week, but I finally got the email with Esmarelda's background check. It was the first time I learned Esmarelda's full name, her age, and where she was from, which happened to be San Antonio, Texas. Mother had told us Esmarelda was from Spain. That was odd, but I could brush that off as a misunderstanding. What I couldn't set aside was that, according to the report, Esmarelda's Social Security number was associated with five different people with completely different names.

Her work history was spotty. She'd been employed by a couple of medical agencies and a hospital but didn't have any medical or nursing credentials. She'd worn scrubs often when she was with Mother, so I suppose I assumed she had some medical training. Maybe, though, that was how she made her clients feel more comfortable and a way to build trust. Without any medical training, it was clear to me that Esmarelda only had experience to be Mother's cook, housekeeper, and chauffeur to doctor appointments and running errands.

Another interesting thing the background check revealed was that she'd moved all over Dallas County, back and forth several times from the northeast side to the southwest side. The county is 908 square miles. It's not like she was moving across town. I started to form a theory. Had she moved so much because she'd burned bridges with other clients and their families and had to leave? What other reason would cause a person to move around so much?

The next section of the report contained Esmarelda's legal history. She'd been associated with several civil actions on record such as overdue tax bills and rental delinquencies, and buried within the history, I found a mention of an arrest and jail time for a DUI.

The report included data derived from my mother's 2001 Lexus VIN, presenting a table of locations, dates, times, and frequencies. This table documented the vehicle's presence at Esmarelda's residence in Desoto, various local sites, and even Austin, nearly 200 miles from Dallas. While intriguing, what that list meant wasn't quite clear to me. I decided to set it aside for another day.

Weeks went by; the background check remained a cold, unsettling weight. My half-hearted online searches yielded nothing—just a dull echo in the vast digital void. Then, an email arrived, purported to be from Mother, though by then, her relationship with technology was tenuous at best. She said she was going to disburse the generation-skipping trust (GST), something my grandmother had set up in her will. Mother had been the trustee of the GST. A logical step, I told myself, because I figured

Mother had decided she couldn't manage the accounts like she had in the past.

Looking back, I can only shake my head at my naive reasoning. A master class in self-deception. First, Mother, even in her decline, was a force of nature, a narcissist to her core. Admitting weakness, especially regarding her precious finances, was anathema. Second, this "generosity" was a calculated maneuver, a ploy. She and Esmarelda, it seemed, believed a payout would appease us, sending us scurrying back into our corners.

The email, a cold, clinical document, outlined the procedure: Contact Moe's office, provide banking details, and the funds would materialize within the week. Liquidation of assets would be a necessary step. Wendy and I were to receive our shares directly, while our brother, deemed less fiscally responsible, would have his shares managed through an account at Moe's firm. He had always had some challenges with handling money, so I figured this was Mother's way of trying to help him be more responsible.

After calling Mother to thank her for the trust, we chatted briefly then hung up. A week or so passed, and then early one morning, Wendy's name lit up on my phone. In a frantic voice, she said, "Mother is living in a hotel!"

9

—·—

THE FLOOD

SEPTEMBER 2019

"What do you mean, Mother's in a hotel?" I chuckled. I really thought Wendy was joking when she called me with this latest development.

"Why are you laughing? I'm serious. Mother's condo flooded. She had to move out because of all the damage."

"What? No. That's crazy. How did it happen? When did it happen? Where is she now?"

"Thursday morning. I don't know exactly what happened except that she told me she walked from her bedroom to the bathroom and the carpet was wet under her feet."

"Wait, you said this happened Thursday morning? Wendy, it's Sunday. Why didn't you tell me sooner?"

"Because Mother just told me. I called to see how she was doing."

Mother and I didn't speak regularly, not like her and Wendy. I wouldn't put it past our mother to leave me out of the loop. But Wendy? No. She would've told her as soon as it happened. So why didn't she? Why didn't Esmarelda?

"I can't believe no one told us."

"I know. I told her I'd come down to help out, and she started yelling at me," Wendy said.

"Yelling?"

"Yeah. She told me not to come. 'There's no room for you,' is what she said. Her exact words."

"What hotel is she staying in?"

"A Hilton somewhere. I really meant it when I said I'd come down to help, but since she's acting that way, I guess I won't."

How could there be no room for us at a hotel with other rooms? Even if that hotel was full, we could find another one.

"I'll call her this afternoon and see what's going on," I told Wendy.

I wanted to call Mother right away, but these days it took some prep work to have a conversation with her. By prep work, I mean I had to psych myself up to do it. Since Dan moved out and Esmarelda became a daily fixture in her life, her impatience with her children had grown greater. The conversations she had with us could turn antagonistic on a dime. Each time I spoke to her, I tried to do so without expectation because I never knew what mood she'd be in.

I decided to wait until after lunch to call her.

When I finally called, and she answered, I immediately could tell she had me on speaker. She sounded far away, and I could hear ambient noise. She talked loudly to make up for the distance between the speaker and her mouth. I also knew if she were using her phone's speaker that Esmarelda or one of her daughters was near her and most certainly listening to our conversation.

"Mother, Wendy told me your condo flooded? Where are you?"

"I'm in a hotel in Addison."

"Addison? That's pretty far from your condo. Why are you there?"

Addison was at least thirty minutes away. With many hotels near her condo, I couldn't understand why she was so far from her home.

"It's where the insurance company sent us," she replied nonchalantly. *We*, meaning Esmarelda. Hearing her refer to Esmarelda and her as "we" grated on my nerves. These days, Esmarelda pretty much provided 24/7 in-home care for Mother.

"Tell me what happened."

"I woke up to go to the bathroom, and I discovered the carpet was wet. The toilet had overflowed. Water had gotten into the closet, the other bathroom, and through the wall to the den."

Mother's explanation made no sense to me. The bathroom she referenced was more than ten feet deep, with the toilet positioned in the back corner. I couldn't understand how water from an overflowing toilet could travel so far that it made its way into the den. Also, how could there be so much water that the damage was bad enough Mother had to leave the condo? It seemed impossible for a toilet overflow to cause the kind of widespread damage Mother described. The scale of the "disaster" felt exaggerated, a convenient excuse to get her out of the condo. It was just a feeling then, but as I sat with the details, I started to believe this wasn't an accident. This was a lie.

"Was Esmarelda with you when you went to use the bathroom?"

I remembered Wendy telling me a few months earlier that Mother had been needing help getting to and from the bathroom. She told Wendy that Esmarelda sometimes wouldn't help her after she'd gotten in and out of bed several times, which left her managing her toilet needs alone.

Mother didn't answer me. Instead, she said, "They told us not to go back into the condo."

"Who's *they*, and why did *they* say that?"

"The management team. Some of the wood flooring in the den is pulled up, and I tripped on it while walking around. So, they said not to come back until it's fixed. Esmarelda's been staying in touch with the insurance company and going back and forth to the condo and bringing things here." I found it hard to believe someone could tell you to leave the condo you owned, especially for something as what I perceived should've been minor water damage.

Something else bothered me about the situation. I knew Mother trusted Esmarelda, but I didn't like the idea of her handling things for her. I simply didn't trust her.

"How long will it be until you can move back home?"

"I don't know; it could be weeks. The insurance company is looking for a temporary place for me to live. I'm hoping they find a place near the Athena."

"Do you need me to come down and help?"

"No." The word landed like a sledgehammer. "There's no room for anyone else here."

It was very clear from the shortness of her answer that she absolutely didn't want me there. There was no use arguing with her. I wasn't going to get any further with her than Wendy had.

"Okay, well, I'll check back in with you later. Please, if you need anything at all, call Wendy or me."

"Okay."

With that, she hung up.

I ended the call feeling uneasy and guilty. Should I have pushed harder? Was it right for me to let my elderly mother handle such a situation on her own? But she wasn't really alone, I told myself. She had people around her. Larry checked in on her. She was in a hotel with staff that she could ask for help when she needed it. The insurance company handling her claim she'd been with for years, and an old family friend from Mother's church ran it. I figured they'd take good care of her.

Still, I felt I needed to do more. I knew Mother's health would continue to decline, but I didn't understand at that time just how much help she would need as the dementia worsened. I knew she would need people around her more and more, people with the education and training to handle her health issues—not an in-home caretaker who didn't have a nursing or skilled care background.

But Mother loved Esmarelda. I realized at this point that Esmarelda was a person who, in her eyes, could do no wrong. It seemed to me that Mother trusted Esmarelda's care and guidance more than her children's. She had put her trust in a stranger, who knocked on her door one day, more than the people who loved and cared for her their whole lives—her family.

The water damage in Mother's condo had gotten me thinking about something I discussed with her in March of 2018 when we visited her over Kelsey's spring break. A longtime friend of Mother's lived in an assisted living facility, a senior community. I'd taken Mother there for a tour and suggested she might consider downsizing. She didn't need such a big place for herself. It would eventually get too much to handle—and wouldn't she like living near her friend?

The apartment in the senior community was nice, a comfortable two-bedroom apartment—enough space for herself, and the second bedroom would make a lovely guest room. Mother sat in the piano room of her home, looked around, and asked what she could keep from the condo.

"Probably very little," I said, and she sobbed.

She couldn't imagine such a thing. How could she get rid of all her belongings? No way would they fit in an apartment half the size of her condo. She couldn't fathom waking up in a strange place. The Athena had been her parents' home, and now it was hers. More than all that, living in the Athena projected an image of class and style, a lifestyle she refused to let go of even if living in such a place didn't suit her current needs.

How would Mother manage in a hotel for several weeks or longer? Perhaps she would do well because she knew it would only be temporary, not a permanent move.

Over the next few weeks, construction continued on the condo. Wendy and I would check in with Mother, but she wouldn't give us much information about the renovations. Neither would anyone else: Larry, Moe, Esmarelda—radio silence. All we knew was she hadn't moved back into the condo. We could only hope the people she'd entrusted to help her were looking out for her. We wouldn't learn of Mother's new living situation until months later, and it would shock us all!

10

— · —

ISOLATED

November 2019-January 2020

I t started with another call from Wendy. Lately, her calls always revealed some new detail about Mother's life that left me shaking my
head. I actually started to dread picking up the phone when my sister's
number flashed across my phone's screen because I never knew what was
coming.

"So, guess what happened yesterday?" Wendy asked the moment I said
hello.

"I haven't a clue." I took a deep breath and braced myself for what was
to come because the blend of exasperation and disbelief in Wendy's voice
prepared me for news I knew I wouldn't want to hear.

"I called Mother yesterday, and she told me she has a new home."

"What do you mean 'a new home'?"

"She barely said hello when she answered my call before going right
into telling me she has a new place."

"A new place? She must mean the hotel and is confused."

"No, Chip, a brand-new place. A condo in Turtle Creek. She signed
a year lease."

What the hell? How could Mother make such a decision without at
least talking to us first? It's true we didn't have any say in the matter

legally since we didn't have financial power of attorney, but why wasn't it at least a discussion? Knowing where our Mother was was important to me. I didn't like thinking about her out in the world untethered to us.

"How did she find that place?"

"Want to guess?"

"Esmarelda?"

"Yep. She claims Esmarelda learned about it from a friend at the bank?"

"What friend? What bank?"

"I don't know. That's all she told me."

Since we'd been removed as MPOAs, communication came to us only on a need-to-know basis, which was hardly ever. If Mother didn't tell us something directly, we didn't know about it, and she never seemed interested in telling us anything. She'd always been rather secretive with her private life, but this seemed like something more. She'd feed us tidbits of information, enough to keep us in the know but with as few details as necessary. If Mother wasn't talking to us, that meant she was talking to Esmarelda and her cohorts. I couldn't help but wonder if Esmarelda had told her to limit what she told us.

"But what about the condo at the Athena?"

"She says when the repairs are done, she's going to sell it."

"Sell it?" I couldn't believe Mother would sell that condo. "Do you think she's serious or just attention seeking?"

The dementia made it hard to tell sometimes. Mother always had a degree of attention-seeking behavior throughout her life. She'd say and do things to make sure she stayed the center of attention, sometimes telling half-truths and even outright lies. But I knew her mind wasn't the same as it was even a year earlier. Her dementia made it harder to figure out which person I was talking to: the not-formally-diagnosed narcissistic mother I knew all my life or the one whose mind had started to betray her. It also made it harder to know if the decisions Mother was making were hers or someone else's.

"I think she's serious. She talked about hiring a Realtor."

"Who would she hire? Does she know someone?"

"She says Esmarelda knows someone from Arlington."

Of course Esmarelda would know someone. I had no evidence that Esmarelda would benefit financially from Mother selling her condo, but what I did know was moving to Turtle Creek would further isolate her. Esmarelda would have her all to herself.

Then there was the location of the new apartment, ten miles from the Athena. You might think that's not too far outside her zone of familiarity, but for an elderly woman who didn't have the opportunities to meet new people outside of her current social circle, it was. She knew no one in the new apartment community. Everyone she interacted with daily lived in the Athena or the neighborhood the condo building towered above.

"Someone needs to get down there and figure out what's going on," I said. Yet, with work and family obligations, I knew a visit was out of the question until after the new year. Wendy also had a full schedule. I thought about contacting Esmarelda to learn more about what was happening with Mother's living arrangements, but I had a hunch she wouldn't be forthcoming.

My brother was my one hope.

He visited Mother every Christmas. I figured he could get more information about the move and fill us in, but Christmas came and went, and we knew little more than what Mother had told Wendy over the phone.

"What's the place like?" I asked.

"It's definitely smaller. Just two bedrooms with a den or small office space that had a small foldout couch I slept on."

Why hadn't he slept in the second bedroom? Was Esmarelda using that room?

"How is she doing overall with the move?"

Eric said she seemed fine and settled in. "She's acting a bit older, but nothing out of the ordinary."

I had my doubts. Sometimes, especially when it comes to our parents, we see what we want to see. We don't want to accept anything but normal aging. We don't want to believe the person who raised us is slowly losing their grip on reality, making her vulnerable in a million different ways.

I needed to see Mother in person.

My busy work schedule wasn't lightening up. I couldn't take a few days off right after the holidays, but I could make it down to see her in March. I could also work remotely from her place. The bottom line was this: I needed to make a trip to see her. I booked a round-trip ticket for the middle of March.

Leading up to my visit, I spoke to Mother off and on. The calls were always short—no more than about fifteen minutes—but they were awkward because she had to use her phone's speaker. We could never have private conversations.

Wendy also tried to stay in contact with our mother. She became particularly concerned in mid-January of 2020 when she tried to get ahold of her two afternoons in a row. By Saturday evening, a couple days after trying to call Mother, she called me concerned because she wasn't answering.

"It's just odd," Wendy told me. "Where could she be, and why wouldn't she pick up the phone? She always answers or at least calls back."

I asked her for Esmarelda's number. We had to know Mother was safe. I texted her that evening to find out why Mother hadn't answered her phone.

Me

Hi. Can you tell me what is going on with Joell?

Esmeralda

Hi, you can talk to Joell. She is sleeping and doing great from what I can tell.

Me

I can't talk to her. She won't answer her phone today. That's not normal. Next call will be a wellness check.

Esmeralda

She was out to dinner and seemed fine. If we thought she was not normal, we would take her to her physician. Not to worry.

Me

She is NOT being normal.

Esmeralda

Please talk to her. We don't get in her personal business about her family.

Me

She doesn't avoid phone calls!

Esmeralda

We are here 7 days, 24 hours, and I don't see anything that's not normal about your 80-year-old mother. She may be tired and went to bed early. Eighty-year-old folks do that some-

times. Call her tomorrow. Thanks and have a
good night.

I replied back, telling her we did and hadn't gotten through. Esmarel-da never replied to that text.

Something wasn't right. I felt it in my gut—and, although I didn't know it at the time, years later after Mother's death, I would discover I was correct. March couldn't come fast enough. I needed to lay eyes on my mother and see what was really going on.

Then, two things happened.

First, a text from Mother's phone was sent to me and Wendy. Here's how it read, grammatical errors and all:

Mother (presumably)

Chip and Wendy this is a message for you I want to tell you that I need to not have you come now to see me I'm gonna have things to do that or that are very important and I'm in the middle of some stuff new stuff that I've never had before so I don't want company so I will call you when I'm ready thank you.

The text seemingly referred to mine and Wendy's separate sched-uled visits in March. What could Mother possibly have going on that wouldn't be handled within the next several weeks?

I couldn't understand why Mother wouldn't want us there and why she had begun to pull away from us, making it more difficult than it already was to communicate with her. I didn't care what she wrote. I had every intention of visiting in March.

But more than that, the text message itself seemed deeply out of char-acter. It wasn't that Mother texted often, but when she did, her messages made sense. She was a woman whose pride in being put-together wasn't limited to her clothes and jewelry; it extended to her every communication. The text on my phone was a grammatical train wreck. Mother would never have used the word "gonna." But you know who would? Esmarelda. I felt certain Esmarelda had written the text, desperately hoping to keep us from visiting.

If she wrote that text, she got her wish. Because shortly after, the world shut down.

11

—·—

SHUTDOWNS

MARCH 2020

W e'd heard rumblings a few weeks earlier of a virus spreading through Asia and Europe. Yes, you know the one I'm talking about, the coronavirus, or COVID. Foreign governments were shutting down borders, restricting movement, and demanding people isolate themselves in place for their health and safety to stop the spread of a deadly virus. By the first week of March in the United States, we still had freedom of movement. I never once believed our government would do anything as drastic as the Asian and European countries. How wrong I was!

"They're thinking of locking down the apartment building," Mother told me over the phone one night. "The building manager isn't letting people in the hallway unless they're going to the garage. You can't come down, Chip."

"What? How? Management can't tell you where you can and can't go in your building."

"I don't know. But that's what's happening."

My veins thrummed with raw frustration. I'd been looking forward to this trip for months. I had to get face-to-face time with Mother. Esmarelda's influence on her had proven too great. Since the end of February,

CHARLES E. WALLACE JR.

it seemed I could only reach my mother by going through Esmarelda first. Any time I called, she answered the phone and would then pass it to Mother. I tried telling myself maybe it wasn't as bad as I was making it out to be. Yet what stayed on my mind and kept me up at night was thinking maybe it was worse. I needed to be with her to get to the bottom of what was really going on.

But what could I do? If I couldn't get into the building, I couldn't lay eyes on the apartment and Mother's living situation. I called the airline the next day, explained the lockdown situation at Mother's apartment building, and they issued me a flight credit that was good for twelve months. I'd have to wait until this COVID thing blew over. It couldn't last that long, could it? Little did we know, right?

Meanwhile, Mother remained isolated. She had no family, close friends, or even acquaintances nearby. At the Athena, she knew many of the residents and all the building staff. At the Turtle Creek apartment, she only had Esmarelda.

She did continue regular communication with her doctors and went to visits when permissible. Esmarelda took her. She'd also begun regular physical therapy sessions at one point, which I was overjoyed to learn.

As the weeks passed, our conversations became fewer and fewer, with her relaying less and less information about her health or even her daily life. When I called, she seemed increasingly out of it and unable to hold a long conversation. Most of our phone calls lasted less than ten minutes, a huge change from the times we could have a thirty-minute conversation. I had to repeat myself often because she couldn't understand me. I could also hear Esmarelda in the background prompting her to answer my questions.

Communicating with Mother had become much more difficult, but that wasn't the only issue. We also had problems getting any information or updates on her condition. Since being removed from the MPOA,

Wendy and I were in the dark about her health. I felt like Mother had to have confided in Esmarelda about her health. So why wasn't Esmarelda relaying that information to us—her family?

We had no clue how Mother was doing, and each time an opportunity in 2020 came about for one of us to visit, we were prevented from coming.

There's COVID on my floor.

No visitors are being let in.

You can't come.

At the beginning of April, Wendy received a text message from Mother's phone after several days of phone calls to her went unanswered.

Joell (presumably Esmarelda)

> *Joell requested we let you know she does not feel like talking. States "Hope everyone is well. Love Mother."*

Wendy

> *Thanks for this. Is Joell well?*

Joell (presumably Esmarelda)

> *Yes, she is well. Joell is a warrior she does not crumble easily. Thank God for her strengths. Stay safe!*

Wendy

> *Just please keep her home. Thank you.*

The texts, though seemingly a bit better grammatically, had the same ring to it as the text Mother sent to us in January when she told us not to visit. Had Esmarelda written that text too?

By now, it was clear to me that Esmarelda had been writing Mother's responses—but were they really my mother's words? Mother didn't use phrases like "hope everyone is well."

With so much pushback and the endless social distancing regulations, Wendy and I decided to wait it out. To say it was frustrating is an understatement. We tried to stay in contact with more frequent phone calls, but we couldn't get much information from Mother. She always told us she was fine when we asked. She talked about physical therapy and refusing to get the vaccine, or "one of those shots," as she called it. This drove Wendy nuts. Mother was particularly excited one time when talking to Wendy about the soup Esmarelda had made for her. Mother clearly continued to be smitten with Esmarelda, and my suspicions of her influence continued to grow, especially as the year went on and communication became less and less.

I felt like the pandemic created the perfect storm, the perfect conditions for Esmarelda to finally isolate our mother from us for her personal gain. From March 2020 through the first half of 2021, we heard less from Mother. It wouldn't be until June 2021 that we found out her living situation had changed again.

12

— · —

ASSISTED LIVING

June 2021-January 2022

I should have been used to Wendy calling with surprises regarding Mother, but when she called in June 2021 to tell me our mother had moved into an assisted living facility, it floored me.

"Are you joking? Mother told me she'd never do that." I remembered how upset Mother had been years earlier when I'd mentioned it to her as an option. "What caused the move? Is it a memory care facility?"

"I don't think so. It sounds like it's a one-bedroom apartment, and I don't know why she's there."

"Well, maybe that'll be better for her. She'll have more help, and we can finally be rid of Esmarelda."

"Not quite. She told me she's going to keep employing Esmarelda and the others."

The others meaning Esmarelda's helpers, I assumed. I didn't like this new development one bit. Everything with Mother seemed to happen suddenly and behind our backs.

"Someone needs to get down there to see her, but work is busy. What's your schedule like?" I asked Wendy.

"I have some time available in early August. I could go then."

It bothered me that we'd have to wait weeks for answers, but that seemed to become the norm. Besides, we weren't in charge of the decisions Mother made. She'd made it perfectly clear that role no longer fell to us. We also couldn't drop everything at a moment's notice every time some new development came to light. We had our lives to manage as well. I often felt bad about not being so readily available, but I knew we weren't the only family facing this type of situation. As much as I distrusted Esmarelda, I felt I had no choice but to let her handle things.

Over the next few weeks, before Wendy made the trip to Dallas, I called Mother a few times. Each time I called, I tried to find out more about what life was like at the assisted living place, which I learned was near the Athena. At least she made it back to her old neighborhood. That made me feel a little better. I would ask her what activities she did during the day. I asked for information about her health. Mother never really answered my questions. All I could gather from those calls was she sounded like she was growing more feeble by the day. Her voice sounded weaker. She tended to lose track of the conversation. She sounded tired.

One bit of information I did get from her was she'd found a buyer for her Athena condo. Finally, I thought. The repairs had been done, and the condo had been listed for over a year with little interest from buyers. She couldn't convey any information to me about the upcoming sale, like how much it sold for and when closing would happen. So, I went to Realtor.com to see what I could find out.

The price history showed the asking price had consistently been lowered, eventually selling for $25,000 less than the original price. What really caught my attention were the photos of Mother's place. The photos featured modern furniture clearly photoshopped in. I know many real estate agents do this to give buyers an idea of what the home could look like when the house no longer has furniture in it. Photoshopped furniture is cheaper than renting furniture to stage the place.

But that left me with one question: Where did all of Mother's stuff go?

I never asked that question back then, which would prove costly in the future. Instead, I got distracted by Mother's condition after Wendy's visit.

"Mother looks so old," Wendy told me.

"Well, she is old," I replied.

"No, not like that, Chip. She doesn't even look like herself. It's like she's aged ten years overnight. She's thinner than ever, which is really saying something. She needs a walker to get around and isn't participating in any activities offered at the facility."

Wendy went on to tell me that while she visited, she took our mother to an art class. She said Mother seemed to enjoy it. So she asked Esmarelda why she wasn't doing these sorts of things under her care.

"Your mother doesn't want to do anything," Esmarelda had told her. "We can't make her do any of these classes if she doesn't want to."

Wendy had told Esmarelda she needed to try harder. "She's dying and looks awful."

"We're doing the best we can," is how Esmarelda replied.

Wendy told me Mother was in such a state that she was convinced she wouldn't see her alive again.

13

— . —

LAST VISIT

December 2021

About a week before Eric's annual Christmas visit to see our mother, we learned she'd been placed on hospice.

"How much time do you think she has?" I asked Eric.

"I don't know. Maybe three or four months? She moves really slow and is so thin. She spent most of the time in a recliner in front of the television. She barely speaks, and when she does, it's so soft."

I wanted to believe Eric was exaggerating, but I knew he wasn't. Usually, he gives vague reports. He leaves out obvious details and is just generally bad with information. For him to have given me that much information unprompted, I figured she must be pretty bad.

It was time for me to visit Mother, maybe for the last time.

I made arrangements to visit her over a long weekend at the end of January. I tried calling her a week or so before my trip on two separate occasions to let her know of my plans. No one answered the phone either time. I left two messages. Neither was returned. I decided I'd show up and see what happens.

Upon my arrival at the facility, I checked in at the front desk. COVID protocols were still in place, so I had to have my temperature taken before I could go to Mother's room. After being cleared, a staff member led me to the elevator and took me to the sixth floor. I couldn't go by myself because the elevator to the residential floors required a resident card or a staff key.

Mother's apartment was two doors down from the elevator. As I approached her apartment, I noticed her door was slightly ajar, and I could hear the television playing loudly. It sounded like a violent movie. I nudged my way in without knocking. I had no clue what to expect.

Once I had the door fully open, I found myself standing in the kitchen, which opened to a sitting area with a couch, a coffee table, and an electric recliner. Mother sat in the recliner facing the television. The television sat on a stand in the middle of the wall with a couple of clear plastic shelves underneath the stand that housed the wireless router and other miscellaneous electronic devices.

The first thing I thought was, How much time does she spend in that chair watching loud, violent television? I couldn't remember her ever wasting her days in front of the television.

As I made my way further into the room, I saw a caregiver sitting on the far side of the couch. It startled me a bit because I wasn't expecting anyone else in the room with her. I didn't know this caregiver, but I wasn't surprised. Over the last three years, Esmarelda and Larry had told me virtually nothing about Mother's life, and Mother wasn't particularly forthcoming with information either.

I nodded at the caregiver and surveyed the room's contents. Several pieces of Mother's furniture dotted the room. On the end tables were lamps from Mother's Athena condo. She always had so many lamps, some she'd selected but others handed down from her mother and one of her previous mothers-in-law. I used to joke that the volume of lamps was so great that if you tripped anywhere in the condo, you would take out no fewer than three lamps.

Even with all the lamps, the room felt dark and cold, devoid of Mother's personality. It seemed someone had tried to decorate the space with a mixture of Mother's decorative items and some discount store figurines. I assumed Esmarelda had chosen the decor. The mother I knew wouldn't have chosen such kitschy items. Her tastes were always more refined.

I did notice the self-portrait of Mother she loved so much. As usual, it was in a central location so you'd see it immediately, but it surprised me to see Christmas lights draped over it, reminding me of the painted portraits of desert scenes in the hole-in-the-wall Mexican restaurants I'd visited throughout Texas during my visits. How tacky! I could only imagine Esmarelda or another caretaker had hung them over the painting. I already had a strong distaste for Esmarelda and the whole situation. Seeing those lights only made the distaste even more bitter.

Mother didn't notice me until I stepped beside the recliner.

"Hi," I said loudly so she could hear me over the loud television.

She smiled at me. Her expression expectant.

"Did you know I was coming to visit?" I asked her.

She nodded.

"Did they tell you how long I'm staying?"

"For the weekend," she whispered. It seemed even more difficult for her to speak since the last time we talked.

"Actually, I'll be here through lunch on Monday," I told her as I settled in on the couch opposite the caregiver, introducing myself as I sat down.

Mother continued to watch her television show, seemingly not interested in a conversation. So I spoke with the caregiver, trying to get a clearer understanding of how things worked there.

"So, what do you guys usually do in the evening?"

"Well, dinner is around 5:30 p.m., and then she usually watches television until around seven."

"What happens after seven?"

"It's bedtime. I call the front desk and ask for an assistant to come up and help get your mom out of the chair and down the hall and into bed."

"She goes to bed around eight?"

"Yes."

"What time does she get up?"

"I get her up around eight the next morning."

Twelve hours in bed. That seemed excessive. I wondered if Mother slept the whole time or if she watched television or read.

"What is her morning routine?"

"Well, like in the evening, I will call for assistance again to get her out of bed. Then we bathe her, get her dressed, and she comes out here to her chair and eats her breakfast. She's usually done with breakfast around 9:30 a.m."

I glanced over at Mother. She continued to watch television, either unaware of our conversation or not caring about it. It broke my heart to think of her sitting in that chair all day, every day. I stayed with her until she went to bed that evening and told the caregiver I'd be back the next day after breakfast.

When I returned the following morning, I spent most of the visit sitting on the couch while Mother sat in the recliner. I tried showing her photos on my phone of her granddaughters and our house. She'd never seen our current house since we moved. I tried to convince her to come visit a few times in 2019. At that time, she seemed capable of making the trip. I even told her she could bring Esmarelda, but she refused. She claimed getting in and out of the airport was too difficult. Maybe a wheelchair would make it easier, I had suggested. She rejected that idea, which didn't surprise me at all.

Mother didn't seem too interested in the photos of the girls and the house. So I found an old photo album with photos from a cruise Mother and Dan had gone on in 2000. They'd gone on several European cruises throughout the course of their marriage. Traveling was a shared passion they had. I thought maybe she'd enjoy going down memory lane.

While we were looking at the album, Esmarelda showed up wearing not one but two surgical masks. She burst through the apartment's front door, carrying a single grocery bag overflowing with paper products. She plunked the bag down on the counter. She didn't say hi. Didn't ask how we were. Instead, she said, "You're not wearing a mask? I've tested positive at least twice."

I resisted rolling my eyes at Esmarelda's excessiveness.

"We're okay here," I said, turning my attention back to the photo album.

As I turned one of the pages in the middle of the book, a packet of old photos slid out. I recognized the photos immediately. They used to be in a green leather binder with plastic protective pockets attached to each page and contained childhood photos of Wendy and me. Where was that album? Actually, where were all the boxes of old photos and school yearbooks? I hadn't seen any of those boxes in this small apartment. It reminded me of the unasked question I'd had when I found out Mother had moved into this apartment.

"Esmarelda, where are Mother's things? Like her photo boxes and other furniture items?"

"Oh, your mother had us get rid of everything," she said dismissively.

"Everything? That's impossible." I couldn't fathom that. No way Mother had gotten rid of everything, especially those photo boxes. Throw away pictures of when she was young? Esmarelda had to be exaggerating. The thought was so absurd it was almost comical, but the empty space in the apartment told me perhaps it wasn't. Someone had certainly gotten rid of most of Mother's belongings.

"Well, there are a few pictures and mirrors left. They're in a small storage room."

I couldn't believe it. There was no way all the boxes of photo albums and school yearbooks were gone. Those were the artifacts of my childhood that detailed our lives. How could they have just disappeared?

"Are you sure it's all gone?"

"Yes." And then, almost daringly, she said, "You can call Larry and ask him."

I sat across from Mother with a decision to make. I wanted to make a fuss and question Esmarelda more, but I didn't think I'd get far. Esmarelda had a way of clamming up and disappearing when I asked too many questions she didn't want to answer. I decided I would do some investigating on my own, waiting until Esmarelda left for the day and then nose around Mother's bedroom and closet to see what was left.

After Esmarelda left, I excused myself from the living room and went into Mother's bedroom. I video-called Wendy so she could also be a part of the investigation.

I stood in front of Mother's jewelry cabinet with the camera facing the drawers.

"Open each drawer and show me what's inside," Wendy said.

I opened each drawer, growing more and more aggravated with what I found—or didn't find, for that matter.

"That's all her old junk and fake jewelry!" Wendy exclaimed.

"Well, maybe she put all the good stuff in the box at the bank," I said hopefully.

"Maybe," Wendy replied. She didn't sound very hopeful at all.

Something wasn't right about this situation. I know Mother had changed a lot over the years as her dementia worsened, but I couldn't imagine her giving nearly everything she owned away. Mother valued her things more than she valued her relationships. Her things defined her. I had a hunch Esmarelda wasn't telling me the full story, but I was afraid to rock the boat. I didn't want to tip her off to my suspicions and make the situation worse, whatever the situation was, because I still didn't know exactly what was transpiring.

As I sat in my mother's apartment contemplating my options, a grim thought entered my head: She doesn't have much longer.

I didn't want to admit the end was near, but she wasn't eating much, drank very little, and was just so very frail. It seemed better to focus on the time left with her, especially since I lived so far away, and leave the rest until a later time.

Turns out, I wouldn't have to wait long. Mother would be gone six weeks later.

14

— · —

THE END, THE BEGINNING

MARCH 2022

Mother died on March 8, 2022. She was not surrounded by her family, but Esmarelda was there. She witnessed my mother's last breath. I know little to nothing about my mother's last days or moments because even after her death, Esmarelda stayed quiet. She hadn't even delivered the news to us. I learned of my mother's passing from a phone call from Wendy telling me she'd gotten "the call" she'd feared from Larry.

What I do know is that following my mother's death from an illness that robbed her of her memories and physical functions, I would learn just how much the woman entrusted to care for our Mother had stolen from her. How much others Mother trusted were either complicit in Esmarelda's scheme or manipulated by her to participate unknowingly in her con. The weeks, months, and years following my mother's death would open up a Pandora's box of deceit that had been hidden under our noses the entire time.

Mother's death didn't bring closure. It only opened the door to a deeper tragedy: a paper trail of stolen money, a shattered estate, and the chilling realization that the person in charge of her care had taken her for a ride.

Laying our Mother to rest wasn't the end. No, it was only the beginning.

PART TWO

UNCOVERING THE TRUTH

15

A NEW CAR, MISSING PAPERS, AND PLENTY OF DOUBTS

MARCH 2022

Here we are. Back where we started at the beginning of the book. I'm in Dallas, reeling from the shock of the empty storage container, standing in the middle of Mother's assisted living apartment trying to piece the last few years of her life together and trying to figure out what went wrong. Seeing that empty storage unit shook me so badly, but I don't know why it did, especially not after what I learned leading up to the trip.

It started with the discovery of a new will Mother supposedly created on January 24, 2020, where she'd willed $300,000 to Esmarelda—the signature written, illegibly, on a mere jagged line. January 24? Why did that date seem familiar to me? It took me a bit to remember the weird text exchanges Wendy had had with Mother around that time in January. It was around that time that Mother had told Wendy and I not to come to Dallas to visit her, after the tickets had been bought. Interesting, I thought when I learned about the new will. It seemed rather suspicious to me that all of a sudden Mother didn't want us to come visit. Also, by January 2020, her cognitive abilities had severely declined. How could she have been in the right mind to make such a change to her will?

Then there was the list Larry had given us showing a $250,000 annuity for Esmarelda. There were more concerning financial discoveries, too, that we'd question and learn more about in the coming weeks and months, but first there were the physical details of Mother's life before her death that needed our immediate attention.

"This is not your mother's place," Rachel said when we walked into Mother's assisted living apartment.

She was right. I had thought the same thing when I visited Mother for the last time at the beginning of the year. The one-bedroom apartment was dark and cold, quite the contrast from her three-bedroom, three-bath condo on the fourth floor of the Athena. It seemed more like a criminal's hideaway than a cozy retreat—and it probably was.

"Let's get the car," Rachel suggested gently, sensing my unease.

I nodded, gripping the keys to my Mother's last car in my palm tightly. In December 2019, she had, apparently, traded in her beloved silver 2001 Lexus sedan with light-colored leather seats and the low mileage one would expect from an owner in her seventies for a brand-new red Lexus. We knew nothing about this new car and were shocked that she'd bought it. Aside from it being a waste of money because her current vehicle worked fine, the basic features and beige interior were things that Mother would have recoiled from. But you know who would've loved the new car? Esmarelda. It fit her tastes to a T.

Mother had actually stopped driving in 2017 when she started to not remember where she was and why she had left her condo in the first place. I remembered Wendy telling me that, and I figured it was something age-related, even though it was weird that she'd lived in the same community most of her adult life and started having trouble getting around. Still, I didn't connect the confusion to the possible first signs of dementia.

In 2018, when Esmarelda began working for Mother, the 2001 Lexus that once sat in the condo's parking garage undriven found its way back on the road—this time with Esmarelda behind the wheel. Mother let Esmarelda drive it to run errands and to take her to doctor appointments. Eventually, she allowed Esmarelda to take the car home with her and use it to get back and forth to Mother's place, which was about twenty-five miles north of Esmarelda's home. Mother even added her to the car insurance.

The reasoning to let Esmarelda use the car made some sense, but not for my mother. I remember thinking it was strange how much she trusted Esmarelda because trusting a stranger (which Esmarelda pretty much still was at that time) with driving her much-loved silver Lexus wasn't something Mother would do. She loved her material items so much more, it seemed, than her relationships. So what was different with Esmarelda?

I always had a feeling Esmarelda was taking advantage of Mother, but I never had proof, only that gnawing feeling that something wasn't right. I was grateful for Esmarelda's caregiving since my siblings and I lived so far away, but some things weren't adding up. Like the time during the summer of 2018 when Mother called me to tell me she and Esmarelda had gone on a road trip to a casino in Oklahoma.

"You went on a road trip?" I had seen my mother a few months earlier, and no way would I have taken her on an overnight road trip. By that time, her mental and physical decline had become more pronounced. She shuffled her feet when she walked. She had trouble handling silverware when she ate. Morning activities like getting dressed and brushing her teeth had been more troublesome for her. I couldn't imagine what it would be like to help her manage these tasks away from her condo.

"Yes, and we stayed overnight at a hotel!" Mother's excitement came through the phone. She almost sounded like a young girl, bubbly and giddy over a new adventure.

The conversation left me confused. First, Mother hated casinos. Her loathing of casinos seemed to me to stem from an experience she'd had with her second husband. He loved them, possibly more than her, which drove her nuts. So, for her to be so ecstatic about going on a road trip to a casino seemed completely out of character.

Putting Mother's history of hatred for casinos aside, something else didn't add up. Why would anyone, especially someone who wasn't family, take an elderly woman with dementia on a road trip to a new place? The casino was located across the Red River, two hours north of Mother's town. The only logical conclusion I could come to was this wasn't a new place for Esmarelda to visit. She was likely a regular and could explain the elderly companion without raising any suspicions.

When I told Wendy and Rachel early on about my suspicions that Esmarelda might be taking advantage of Mother, they didn't quite agree. I get it. Esmarelda provided much-needed support that we couldn't give because we lived so far away. What would we do without Esmarelda? That seemed to be the general feeling by everyone, including me at times.

Still, my suspicions gnawed at me. I kept bringing up my concerns, which were frequently met with these words: What proof do you have?

At the time, I had no proof, but it would come in the worst possible ways—one of those ways was the discovery of the red Lexus.

I was convinced when I saw the brand-new red Lexus that it was never meant for Mother. Esmarelda had used my mother's money to buy that car for herself. Another convincing factor was the mileage on the new Lexus, which was only two years old in 2022. By this time, Esmarelda had been living with Mother around the clock five days a week. If the car was only being used for errands during the week and being driven back to

Esmarelda's on the weekends, I surmised the car should only have about ten to twelve thousand miles on it. Maybe fifteen thousand, at the most. When I checked the mileage, it had over twenty-four thousand miles put on it in two years.

But it wasn't the car that shifted my suspicions into overdrive. It was the safe-deposit box. The day after we got the keys to Mother's car, I drove her Lexus to meet with Larry at Chase Bank, a place I knew very well. It was a couple of blocks from Mother's assisted-living apartment, but it had been a part of my life much longer than a couple of years. I used to visit the bank with my grandmother as a young boy, always in awe and mesmerized by how many lock boxes could fit in the space, floor to ceiling.

The last time I'd been to the bank was when I visited Mother in September 2018. We went to the bank one afternoon, and she requested I be added to the safe-deposit box signer list. The box had been in the family for decades, first rented by my grandmother on July 11, 1947. I always remember the month and day because it's the same as my firstborn's birthday. At that time, the box had contained my grandparents' wills, my great-grandmother's marriage license from the early 1900s, and several payoff statements for Mother's previous homes. The box also contained divorce documents from Mother's previous four marriages and an odd scoresheet-like piece of paper listing each former husband and the time frame of the marriage. Weird, but Mother certainly had her quirks.

The box also contained an assortment of jewelry boxes, all different sizes, and my grandfather's Shriners ring, which I hadn't seen since I was eight or nine years old. It was gold with an emerald stone. Touching that ring made me feel connected to my grandfather once again after he'd been gone for so long. That feeling brought a smile to my lips.

"Hey," I said to Larry when I met him inside the bank.

He acknowledged me, but I noticed he wasn't his usual chatty self. He'd been standoffish with me since I had met him at the storage facility. He stayed relatively quiet while we had our IDs validated and entered our PIN numbers to get into the box. After the bank associate confirmed our identification, we walked into the vault, around a large island with safe-deposit boxes, and then around two more walls of floor-to-ceiling boxes. It took us a moment to find the safe-deposit box, but after a short time hunting, we found it two rows down from the top. Larry handed the associate the key; the banker unlocked the box from the wall then handed us the box.

"There are a couple of cubicles on the other side of that wall," he told us, pointing back over his right shoulder.

"Thanks," I said, taking the box from him with both of my hands. It felt lighter than I remembered. As I walked to the cubicle, I tipped the box from side to side. I didn't hear jewelry boxes sliding about, leaving me to assume the box was stuffed with papers.

"Was there a second box?" I asked Larry.

"No, there was only one," he replied indifferently. I got the impression Larry thought I was wasting his time. Yet if he'd done his job while Mother was alive and didn't seemingly conspire with Esmarelda to keep us in the dark, we wouldn't be here needing to check the contents of the safe-deposit box.

I pulled up one of the two chairs in the cubicle to the desk. Larry sat in the other one behind me. As I investigated the box's contents, I began to realize my suspicions of the box containing only papers were true. I pulled out the papers one by one. Some I recognized right away as papers my mother had kept in cabinet drawers at her condo. Panic hit me.

Where were the jewelry boxes? Where were the diamond rings Mother had worn on special occasions? Where was my grandfather's Shriners ring?

As my fingertips touched the bottom of the box, I found something: the package of photos Mother had taken of her condo a few years back for insurance purposes should something happen, like the flood. There weren't photos of the missing jewelry, but I pocketed the photos anyway. They might come in handy somewhere down the road.

Larry and I parted, saying very few words to each other. Him, seemingly ready to be rid of me. Me, in shock, still trying to understand why the jewelry was missing from the safe-deposit box. *What the hell happened?*, I thought during the drive back to Mother's apartment.

Aside from Larry, who'd been Mother's power of attorney and executor of her will, there were Moe and Curly to consider. Were they the ones who put those papers in the safe-deposit box? The papers weren't even safe-deposit worthy. They should've been left in her apartment.

A queasy feeling settled in my gut. I'd never had my home robbed, but if I had, I imagined it would feel like I was feeling now. Walking into the cubicle, finding that what I expected to find in the safe-deposit box was completely gone, felt like being robbed. Which led me to my next thought: Had we been robbed?

I headed back to my mother's apartment to meet the others. Larry came over as well, so he could oversee our work. However, I couldn't get the bank out of my head. I wanted to question him further, make him tell me what he knew because I knew he had to know something. Nothing made sense right now. But I was afraid to put too much pressure on Larry at that moment because of his role as executor of Mother's estate. One wrong move, and he could quit talking to me. I couldn't let that happen because I had questions—specifically, questions about Mother's will.

The will had been given to us the day before. In it, my mother left Esmarelda $300,000 in addition to the annuity. I couldn't believe it! It was out of my mother's character and a complete one-eighty from how she'd previously structured her will, with several trusts established for each of her children. All money was to stay within the family. No charitable contributions. No one-offs to a person here or there. Besides that, I knew my mother. If she wanted to give to charity or someone outside of the family, she would've done that when she was alive for one reason and one reason only: to receive the praise. To give money after she died totally went against her need for attention and accolades.

While the $300,000 to Esmarelda pissed me off, something more concerned me. I couldn't contest the will because of a clause in it stating anyone who contested it could lose rights to any part of the estate. I couldn't take the chance. And probate was going to be expensive. I knew I'd need to hire a lawyer soon, but I'd never hired a lawyer in my life. I made a note to contact Wendy (did I mention she was a lawyer too?), who might have some referrals in Texas for me to contact. What a nightmare!

After the trip to the bank with Larry, I went back to Mother's apartment where my wife and daughter and I were to spend the rest of the afternoon tagging the remaining furniture items and odds and ends, designating what we wanted to keep and what should go to charity. Not much furniture was left in her assisted living apartment. It really shocked me to see how little was left, especially for a woman who once had a collection of furniture expansive enough to fill a three-bedroom, three-bath condo. Where had everything gone? I had questions, and the answers given to me by Larry—that the items were donated to local charities—didn't sit right with me. I needed to speak with Esmarelda.

I had tried contacting her the last couple of days to learn more about the so-called donated items, with no luck. My calls and texts went unanswered, as did Wendy's. While at Mother's apartment, we asked Larry if he could help us get in contact with Esmarelda.

"Let me try her now," he said.

He walked out of the den where we stood and into the bedroom. Why couldn't he talk in front of us? Even more interesting, Esmarelda seemed to pick up within a few rings because we could hear Larry speaking to her. His side of the conversation was mumbled and fairly short. A few minutes later, he walked out of the room and told us she couldn't speak with us now because her daughter was in the hospital.

"What's wrong with her daughter?" I asked.

"She has cancer. She's in the ICU."

"Oh, really? How long has she been there?"

"I'm not sure. Seems like a few days at least."

"So, can we talk to her at all while we're in town?" I had sympathy for her if her daughter was truly in such a state, but certainly she could make some time for us to answer some questions. The fact that she picked up so quickly when Larry called seemed to confirm my suspicions that she'd been dodging my and Wendy's calls.

"If you have any questions, I can pass them along to her," Larry said. Discussion closed. What the hell, I thought. Was Larry running interference now?

After we finished up at the apartment, Larry left, and the three of us went back to our hotel. I opened my laptop to check my email and saw that Larry had forwarded two charity receipts from when Mother's larger storage unit had been emptied in January, the one we'd visited earlier in the week. I opened the first receipt and saw it was from a women's shelter in DeSoto, near Esmarelda's home. The donated items list included a number of boxes along with a few furniture pieces. Nothing seemed out of the ordinary. The receipt included a phone number to the shelter. Maybe they'd still have some of the items donated—specifically, I was interested in the heirlooms and photo albums.

I took a deep breath and dialed the number. A member of the staff answered right away.

"Hi," I began. "I'm calling about a donation made back in January. Some items were donated from my mother's storage unit by her caregiver, and I believe some family heirlooms might have accidentally gotten included in the donation."

"Hmm, I do remember someone bringing us a substantial donation in a large truck. There were lots of boxes."

"Do you still have the donation?"

"It's unlikely." She told me the shelter operated a store and sold items every week, with Fridays being fifty percent off. "Most of our donations don't last long on the sales floor."

"Well, what about photo albums? Did any photo albums come in with the donation, and do you still have them?"

Again, her answer disappointed me. She said they usually emptied donated photo albums and frames and threw away the photos. I shouldn't have been surprised by her answer, but it stunned me. I felt sick to my stomach thinking of our family history just trashed, discarded like it didn't matter. But what could I do? I thanked the staff member and moved on to the next organization Esmarelda "donated" to.

The second organization was located in South Dallas. I didn't recognize the organization's name, but that didn't raise any alarm bells. I wasn't familiar with such organizations in the Dallas area. I'd been living away from Dallas for a long time. The donation receipt listed boxes and furniture as being donated, with the estimated value of the donation about $1,500. The receipt's footer included the usual charitable verbiage about the organization's IRS filing status. Not unusual, but upon further inspection, I noticed the group's name was misspelled. The word *community* was missing an "m." Sure, typos can happen, but on an official receipt, I found it odd that the organization misspelled its name.

Out of curiosity, I opened Google Maps and decided to take a "virtual" drive. I put in the address. It was located in a somewhat seedy area. Online, I navigated past the address and could see from the Google images a boarded-up building. I checked the date on the map and saw the photos were updated within the last couple of months. I navigated around the back of the building. I didn't see any doors or other evidence that the building had once been a legitimate store. An image that popped up that did catch my attention was an opened, heavy-looking gate leading to a door. The next building had a small loading dock located in the back of the building, and the image included photos of two guys handling furniture from the "store" to a small truck.

"What the heck," I said under my breath. "Is this a fencing operation?"

I could hear my wife's voice in my head telling me not to be so suspicious, but I couldn't help it. I'd ignored my gut about Esmarelda's involvement in Mother's life for a long time, and now I was here, searching for missing furniture, family heirlooms, wondering where the contents of the safe-deposit box went to, and actively being avoided by Esmarelda. All of those were good reasons for my suspicions.

I called the phone number on the receipt.

No answer.

I found the organization's email on the receipt and sent an email with my questions about the donations and asked them to get back to me. Next, I did some more internet research. My research led me to the name of the group's president. Another article from a few years earlier detailed how the group's president had been charged with stealing funds from another charity and had assigned her daughter the role of a contractor that came with a very nice salary, paid for by the charity, of course. I continued my research over the next few days, waiting for a response to my email that I'd never get, and found other addresses and phone numbers listed for the Dallas organization. None of the phone numbers worked.

My investigation into the missing boxes and donated furniture distracted me from what needed to be done before heading home: planning Mother's funeral arrangements. Wendy had told me we could hold Mother's service anytime within the next sixty days, since she'd been cremated. I wanted time to go home and come back with a U-Haul to collect what we were keeping from what was left of her belongings. We picked a weekend late in May.

Then Wendy dropped a bomb.

"Guess who's been calling the funeral home, asking when Mother's funeral is and if she can come?"

"Esmarelda?"

"Yup."

"Unreal. She won't answer our calls or texts, but she has the gall to contact the funeral home?"

"Fortunately, they told her it's our decision, the family's, if we want her to know the arrangements."

I didn't want that woman anywhere near Mother's funeral.

"We need to write an obituary for Mother," Wendy told me. "Maybe I should write it."

She chuckled, and so did I. We both knew the type of obituary Mother would want written about her: a glowing recount of her life and all the material things she'd acquired and the acts she completed for others so she'd be heralded in death. We loved our mother, but truth be told, she loved herself more than anyone else.

"I can't wait to read it," I told her.

Before Wendy could write the obituary, she received an email from Larry. It was an email he'd received from Esmarelda, forwarded to him with the subject line "Joell's wish for her obit." Larry wrote in the body of the email, "Here are some notes from Esmarelda."

Esmarelda claimed she and Mother had talked, and the sample obit included key points Mother wanted included. Here's how it read:

Joell Susan Fleming, loving daughter, mother, and friend, passed away peacefully on March 8, 2022. Joell was born October 20, 1939, the only daughter to Dorothy Jo Fisher and Howard Nathan Fink. She graduated from SMU with a Master in Psychology. Joell worked as a teacher and counselor for many years. Joell enjoyed doing volunteer work at Children's Medical and contributed to many charitable organizations. She loved music, travel, and lived a fun-loving life filled with love, generosity, and spiritual peace. Joell will be remembered for her beautiful smile, her soft-spoken demeanor, intelligence, independence, and her unique individuality and strength. She enjoyed a long and sweet friendship and Sunday Brunch with her good friends Lynda Comelius and Stephanie Grimes. She was grateful and fond of her supportive business team Moe Holland, Larry McKibben, and Gail Carron. Joell is survived by three children and three granddaughters.

What was this garbage? Funny how her friends and "supportive" business team were named, but her kids and grandkids were never mentioned by name. Also, the career milestones were exaggerated. She taught first grade for no more than two years before starting a family and staying home. Her counseling gig lasted a couple of years at a middle school and rolled into a part-time marriage counseling gig, which was comical since Mother had a difficult time making her marriages work. The marriage counseling job actually put her in a shared office with an older gentleman, a psychiatrist, who would become her romantic partner following her fourth divorce. She left her job and followed him to a West Texas hospital, where he was the lead psychiatrist for a year before he passed away. Then, she moved back to Dallas, providing caregiving to my cancer-ridden grandmother and volunteering briefly at the local Scottish Rite children's hospital. She quit the volunteer job after meeting Dan, her fifth and final husband.

The obituary's overexaggeration of Mother's accomplishments wasn't entirely out of character for Mother, but not mentioning any of her family by name was. Even though Esmarelda didn't mention herself directly in the obituary, I couldn't help but feel like this sample obituary had been a way to make it seem like we weren't important to Mother and not present in her life. Evidence Esmarelda could use if we contested the will, maybe?

And it turns out, the sample obituary wasn't Esmarelda's first attempt at publishing an obituary. She'd done it before. But I'll get to that later.

16

— • —

ACCOUNTS

APRIL 2022

You can learn a lot about a person when you have access to their cell phone. Oh, the secrets these little handheld computers keep. Mother had two cell phones: an old one and a new one. The old one I had found in its box in her desk drawer when I'd been to Dallas to go through her belongings in March. Mother hadn't been using that phone. She had another that I couldn't find. I'd asked Larry where the phone was, and he told me Esmarelda had it.

Why would Esmarelda have my mother's phone? Larry said Esmarelda had it so she could keep track of Mother's bills. I didn't like this answer one bit. I told Larry I needed that phone, and he assured me he'd get it to me by the following week.

While I waited to receive the current cell phone, I spent some time going through her old phone since it didn't have a password. Luckily, many of the old accounts were still on the old phone. But one odd thing stood out to me. All the old pictures had been deleted. I guess maybe they had been transferred to the new phone. I figured I would see them when the new phone showed up.

The old phone contained Amazon and Netflix apps connected to new email accounts unfamiliar to me. When I opened the phone's email app, I noticed more new email accounts that included variations of Esmarelda's and the other caregiver's name in the IDs. The phone also had an active LifeLock account, a service that provides identity theft protection and credit report information. I had no problem getting into the account because she had saved her user identification, and I was immediately able to pull up a credit report.

I had wanted this information for a couple of weeks by this time and had been waiting on Larry to send it to me. I'd asked him, as the POA and executor of Mother's estate, to pull her credit report. I never received the credit report. Larry claimed tax season kept him busy and he'd get to that little task for me when he had the time. The time never came—until now, when I accessed her report myself.

At first, everything looked normal. The cards, the credit lines, and the payments matched up to what I knew my mother to have: two Citi-branded cards with a combined $40,000 in credit. Then I made it to the bottom of the report. That's where things turned questionable.

A credit card for Belk department store, with a credit line of $2,000, had been opened on January 5, 2021. At first glance, you might think there wasn't reason to be suspicious. The card had been paid on time every month, and the remaining balance was $690, but I knew my mother. First, she didn't fall for in-store credit card sign-ups. She didn't have a wallet full of store credit cards—only her two Citi cards that she'd had for ages. Second, Mother was a retail snob. Never would she ever open up a credit card to a mid-level retail shop. Aside from her retail preferences, the other thing about seeing that store card on her credit report that made the hair on my arms stand up were the location of the stores.

The closest Belk was in a town called Rockwall. At the time the card was opened, Mother had been living in her "new" condo in Turtle Creek, a town nearly thirty minutes west from Rockwall. Why would she open a credit card at a store so far from her home? Mother had never been one to shop too far out of her self-imposed quadrant.

Larry had begun paying Mother's bills since the fall of 2018. At this time, Wendy and I were aware Mother had been having problems holding a pen, and writing checks had become difficult. We had seen a couple of checks come to us over the summer that were obviously not signed by her. So one day, Wendy, trying to protect Mother's financial interests, convinced her to ask her trusted CPA to write the checks for her. I sent Larry a quick email to ask him if he'd ever paid bills to this creditor. Surprisingly, he got back to me quickly and said he hadn't.

His response didn't surprise me. He didn't look at Mother's credit report. All he did was pay the bills he was given every two weeks or so from Esmarelda when he stopped by my mother's house. I began to construct a theory in my mind: Esmarelda opened the account at Belk. She controlled the mail. She opened a credit card in my mother's name to a store near her, hid the statements, and made the minimum monthly payments to avoid collection calls or letters that could alert Mother or Larry to an issue.

But could I prove my theory?

The first step toward proving anything meant calling Belk. I explained to the first person I spoke with at Belk that my mother had passed and I suspected someone had opened her account without her knowledge. The moment I uttered the word "fraudulent," the representative transferred me to the fraud department. Banks don't like to hear that word.

The second rep I spoke with asked me a couple of security questions before moving forward. Fortunately, I had no problems answering these questions. They were simple questions like Social Security number, date of birth, things like that. Once the security questions were out of the way, the representative told me my mother's Turtle Creek address had been used on the initial application and the phone number listed matched an old landline phone number of Mother's. She also told me the account wasn't opened over the phone but at the Rockwall store in January 2021. Yet all the purchases charged to the card were made at a Belk in Waxahachie, a town about fifteen minutes south of Esmarelda's house.

And those purchases?

Well, based on the purchase descriptions the representative gave me, it appeared the clothes weren't for my mother. I deduced these clothing purchases were for individuals living in Esmarelda's household, like her grown children. Most of the purchases were for women's clothing way too big for my mother to wear. She wore a size small. The clothing bought with the credit card included large sizes and some men's clothing. I couldn't think of a single reason for the men's clothing purchases other than Esmarelda buying them for her boyfriend or her daughter's boyfriend.

"Could you send me statements from the account?" I asked the representative.

"I can send you the last few months' worth of statements if that works for you?" It did. She updated the account with my address and immediately froze the account.

"Could you also tell me how the account had been paid?"

"Sure," the rep replied. "It appears the payments were phoned in with payments made using the electronic check option."

"Would you be able to tell me the last four numbers on the account?"

"Of course."

Before hanging up, I asked the fraud department's representative if I could open a case against the person I suspected of opening the account fraudulently for identity theft.

"Unfortunately, in a case like this, no. Since currently there's no outstanding balance, no evidence of fraud or identity theft is apparent."

I shook my head in disbelief. She'd gotten away with opening a card in my mother's name and using it to make unauthorized purchases. I knew they had to be unauthorized because no way my mother would allow Esmarelda to make personal purchases on a card in her name. Even if she had, she wasn't in her right mind to do so. By the time the card had been opened, Mother's dementia had worsened to the point she didn't have the decision-making skills she'd had in the past. The point? Even if Esmarelda had told her about the card and Mother had given her permission, that permission was given with diminished cognitive capacity. Simply put: Mother wouldn't have understood what she was doing.

After the call to Belk, I decided to get into Mother's Wells Fargo account, the account she had consolidated all her accounts into in 2017. I'd had access to the account up until Esmarelda—or even one of her daughters—had helped my mother change the password. How convenient for Esmarelda, right? Now I had to figure out how to get into the account. I had Mother's old cell phone that was connected to her email account. I figured that was a start because any sort of authentication code or two-factor authorization *should* go to that phone.

I pulled up the Wells Fargo site and clicked the "forgot my password" link. A security question popped up: What's your favorite sports team? What luck! Mother had been a lifelong Dallas Cowboys fan. Watching them play games on the holidays and playoffs had been a tradition. That had to be the answer. I typed it in. I breathed a sigh of relief when a new screen popped up and asked me to enter a new password. Some banks ask two or three security questions. I got in with one.

Once I got in her checking account, I began exporting as many statements as I could, going as far back as 2015. I never knew exactly how much money Mother paid Esmarelda, but Wendy had told me in early 2019 she believed Esmarelda was being paid nearly $150,000 a year up to that point for her caretaking services. It was to compensate for Esmarelda's overnight stays—at least, that's what Larry told Wendy when she'd questioned him about it once.

I thought $150,000 was a lot for caretaking, even if overnights were involved, but that number quickly grew once I started reviewing Mother's statements in more detail and inputting checks into an Excel spreadsheet. For three years, it appeared Mother had paid Esmarelda roughly $300,000 a year. I couldn't wrap my head around that number or even justify it. Esmarelda, to my knowledge, had no medical training, no certifications. How the hell had so much money been spent on caretaking services for one person? The only way that happened that I could deduce was Mother had allowed Esmarelda to decide her compensation because she wasn't in a position to say no. When Wendy questioned the amounts, Larry had told her Mother had enough money, so it was okay. Okay for whom? Esmarelda? Larry? Was he getting some kickbacks? No one but the family should've been making financial decisions if Mother couldn't make them herself, but it appeared Esmarelda, with Larry's help, intentional or otherwise, took on this role to her benefit.

While I was in the Wells account, I noticed the method of paying Esmarelda changed in September 2021. Curiously, instead of being paid by check, Larry had started issuing electronic checks through ACH. Because he'd made this switch, I had access to the last four digits of Esmarelda's bank account—and guess what? Those last four digits matched the numbers of the account that had been making the payments on the Belk credit card. Seeing those last four digits match up with the bank account used to make the card payments seemed to support my theory that Esmarelda had been using the card for personal use. But it also left me wondering: If she was making nearly $300,000 a year, why wouldn't she pay off the whole balance? More importantly, if Esmarelda was making well above market rate for her services, why was she receiving pay advances marked as loans?

Yes, Mother, or Larry, rather, was paying Esmarelda advances. In December of 2021, Esmarelda received a $20,000 advance that was to be paid back at $2,000 per check beginning in January of 2022. In addition, the week following my January visit, Larry had written her a $10,000 check as a bonus and for vacation pay. Esmarelda still owed $16,000 for that December advance!

All this money being paid out to a woman who'd over the years began to isolate Mother more and more from us, making every little decision for her because she'd taken our MPOA away from us, didn't sit right with me. Oh, and to top it off, at the end of March 2022, *after* Mother had passed, Esmarelda, who would no longer have what appeared to be an endless flow of income from Mother but still owed $14,000 from the December loan advance, stopped talking to us.

No way was I letting any of this go.

17

— • —

DIVING DEEPER

APRIL 2022

After discovering the Belk credit card account and the loan advances to Esmarelda, I kept digging. How much had Esmarelda taken—dare I say, stolen—from Mother? Since the first week of March 2022, I found three transactions from Mother's bank account. At this point, she was still with us but spent most of her days in bed, weak, lethargic, not eating, and barely drinking. She was what medical professionals call actively dying. She was most certainly not scrolling online and buying things. Yet, someone had made a purchase at an online store that sold loungewear and bedtime clothing for elderly women.

Like I did with Belk, I found the store's number and called them. The mailing address for billing purposes was Esmarelda's home, but the delivery address was Mother's assisted living apartment. The order contained about a dozen pieces of clothing. Only some were Mother's size, an extra small. Before she passed, she'd lost even more weight and averaged about 85 pounds. The remaining items ranged from small to medium, clothing more likely to fit Esmarelda, who was around the same height as Mother but weighed more. The package delivery date was March 9, 2022, the day after she passed.

Sure, I thought, it's possible that Esmarelda had ordered the clothing for Mother a few days prior without anticipating she might pass before they arrived. That wasn't a stretch to consider. But what fanned my suspicions was the package wasn't at the apartment when we arrived on the thirteenth. Rachel suggested Esmarelda might have given them to another client, but I wholly believed the clothes were for Esmarelda, and throwing in a few pieces of clothing for Mother was meant to be a diversion if anyone questioned the purchases.

Two Sam's Club transactions, one on March 3 and the other on March 4, were the next charges that raised an eyebrow. One purchase was made at the Sam's Club by Mother's place. The second purchase had been made at the location near Esmarelda's home. Interestingly enough, these were the first transactions using the Wells Fargo card. Previously, Mother had used her Citi accounts to pay for purchases. As of February 27, 2022, Larry made himself a signer on the two Citi accounts. I began to theorize that Esmarelda had switched to using the Wells Fargo account hoping Larry wouldn't see any of the transactions because those card transactions were often buried at the end of the brokerage statement, making them easy to overlook or ignore, especially if Larry believed only the Citi cards were being used.

I wanted those receipts badly.

I tried logging into Sam's Club with my mother's information. I got in but didn't find what I was looking for. The only activity I found was from months ago at a Sam's Club in Austin, and Dan had made those purchases. Next, I tried the chat option, telling them I was my mother and had allowed someone else to use the account, and I needed to see the receipts. Again, no luck. Esmeralda must have used a different membership card, presumably hers, but paid with Mother's credit cards. I would need Esmeralda's login information to access those receipts, and I didn't have that information.

How could I prove Esmarelda had made those purchases?

A week passed. One night, Rachel and I were out and about running errands in our hometown, hundreds of miles away from Dallas, and we passed the only Sam's Club near us.

Rachel nudged me. "You want to give it a shot?"

She meant did I want to see if someone inside would give me the answers I wanted.

"Sure. Why not?"

I figured one of the advantages of trying to get information in person would be finding a younger, part-time employee, a high schooler or college kid, who didn't know or care about the rules. It took a bit of wandering around, but eventually I found an associate who I hoped would be just that person.

"Hi," I said to the young woman behind the counter. "Could you help me look up my mother's account? She recently passed, and I have some questions about some purchases she made."

"Do you know her phone number?" the associate asked.

"Let's try this one." I read off the numbers of her old landline.

"Looks like that account has been inactive for a while."

That's what I expected to hear. "How about her caregiver's account? Can you look up her information? I really need to get some information about these purchases."

"Yeah, I'll just need the phone number."

I pulled out my phone. I hadn't memorized her phone number just yet, but I had a feeling I'd eventually have it memorized by the time I was done digging.

"Try this number."

I read it out loud. It worked.

"What purchases do you have questions about?"

"I'm looking for two transactions from around the beginning of March 2022."

I gave her the dates and the amounts. She said there were other transactions within that time frame too. She couldn't give me the receipts, but I knew where to go to find them: the brokerage statements.

Trying to unravel what I believed was some serious financial deceit by Esmarelda had become my nightly ritual. I'd become the family detective. I'd planned to continue my scavenger hunt for the receipts to prove Esmarelda had been using Mother's money for personal gain, but the next night when I sat down with the brokerage statements again, something caught my eye—a jewelry appraisal done in December 2020.

What the hell is this? I thought.

Mother had never spoken of having an appraisal done. Any valuables like jewelry should've been in the safe-deposit box. Their disappearance had been a mystery to me when Larry and I visited the bank the previous month. Could this solve the mystery?

I pulled up a copy of the check, signed by Larry. Next, I looked up the jeweler and got their contact information. The place was located up north in an area near Moe's place, one of Mother's fiduciaries. Interesting.

It was late, so I waited until the next day to call the appraiser's office. The woman I spoke with seemed sympathetic and eager to help when I explained the circumstances. She agreed to send me the appraisal report later in the day. When I received the report, I couldn't believe what I read. It wasn't one piece of jewelry that had been appraised. It was $200,000 worth of jewelry! Some of the jewelry had been my grandmother's. Some had been the diamond rings Mother wore. Other pieces I'd never seen. I sent the attachment to my siblings via email.

What do you think of this? I wrote.

My brother, Eric, responded first.

Oh, yeah, Esmarelda sent me some jewelry back in January.
Wendy replied next.
You have to tell us these things when they happen, Eric. Do you have them now?
Yeah. They're in a box in my room.
My brother. He's book smart, but he doesn't think about the logistics of things sometimes. Not thinking to tell us Esmarelda had sent him jewelry was par for the course for him. Also, keeping thousands of dollars' worth of jewelry in a box in his ground-floor rehabbed garage apartment in Los Angeles instead of putting them in a safe or bank box seemed about right for him too.

Can you send us some pictures so we can see what she gave you? Wendy asked.

I wondered why Esmarelda hadn't sent them to Wendy. The best (and more likely answer) was that Wendy would've asked questions. My brother would not.

He sent over the pictures quickly, and we compared them to the appraisal. Several pieces were missing, to the tune of nearly $50,000. One of the missing items was a rather large and extremely gaudy cocktail ring. In the center of the ring was a 3.38-carat deep blue sapphire stone, accentuated by seven round brilliant-cut diamonds, four square euro-cut diamonds, four smaller round blue sapphire stones, five baguette-cut diamonds, and three fancy marquise-cut yellow diamonds that looked like petals or feathers fanning out from the ring. The ring's total weight was approximated to be 7.8 grams, and its replacement value a whopping $20,500.

I had no idea why the appraisal had been ordered. It was something I definitely planned to ask Larry about, but one thing was becoming clearer. Esmarelda Gomez was a methodical thief—and I had a hunch she'd done it before to a man named Bob Barnhill Jr.

Bob Barnhill Jr. never missed a Tuesday night at Goff Burgers, Friday at Kuby's German Deli, or ice cream and cookies after Sunday Mass. He loved a good debate, wasn't afraid of talking politics, and had a dry sense of humor you either got or you didn't. The friendships he acquired over his lifetime were enviable for their quality and sincerity. He was a devout Catholic, worked over thirty-five years in education as a senior health, education, and finance officer, and spent his retirement with his loyal cocker spaniel, Pickles.

Bob passed away in April 2011 at the age of eighty, just a few weeks shy of his eighty-first birthday. According to his obituary, which I found online, he was not survived by any children. Many friends were mentioned in the obituary but no family members. The only mention of family was that some were scattered throughout the United States. Interestingly enough, the obituary mentioned he was survived by a wife and four stepchildren. The wife's name? Well, wouldn't you guess it? Esmarelda Gomez.

Barnhill first showed up on my radar in 2019 when Wendy and I had the background check done on Esmarelda. In the report, it stated Esmarelda had been POA for two men, one in 1998 and another in 2009. She'd even taken the last name of one of the men, Bob Barnhill Jr.

I found this curious and wondered if they'd married. I didn't have a marriage license to prove a marriage or any other proof to back up my suspicions until I found this obituary. There had never been any mention of her being his wife. I clicked through the photos that had been uploaded to his obituary, many of which were of him as a younger man throughout the 1960s. As the photos became more current, Esmarelda and her daughters showed up in them. One was a staged photo with Barnhill in a wheelchair, with Esmarelda and her daughters circling him like one big happy family. It reminded me of photos I'd found on Mother's phone of her and Esmarelda and the daughters.

I can't say for certain that Esmarelda staged those photos with Mother. I can't say for certain that Esmarelda had purposely taken them as a way to prove her relationship with Mother was real and uncoerced. To say, if questioned about why Mother left her so much money, "Why does that seem odd? We had a friendship. Just look at these photos."

I can't prove anything with those photos, but I felt odd when I saw them. Something felt wrong. Just like how Esmarelda's relationship with Barnhill felt wrong—dare I say, transactional. I'd learn more later on about the nature of their relationship when I gained access to thousands of Esmarelda's emails, including that they'd been married a mere three months before his death. But at that moment, with the little amount of information I had, I formed a working theory.

I immediately copied the link to Barnhill's obituary and sent it in an email to Wendy and Eric that contained one sentence: "Looks like we have a prior!"

18

— · —

LAWYERING UP

B etween Wendy, our brother, and me, we had managed to take care of most of Mother's possessions since her passing two months earlier. Still, a few items needed to be gone through and taken back to our respective places. That's why, in May 2022, we met up in Dallas one more time. My son-in-law, Steve, came with me to help.

A few weeks earlier, when everyone had bought their plane tickets, I realized Steve and I would land about three hours before my siblings. I figured we'd just hang out at the airport and wait for them to land. But when we picked up our rental car, a red hybrid Honda Accord with exceptional gas mileage (close to 40 miles per gallon), I realized how much time we had.

"Let's explore a little," I proposed to Steve.

My son-in-law had never been to Dallas before, so he was game for anything. He didn't question me when I gave him two addresses to put in the GPS: the addresses of the shops listed on the charity receipts Larry had given me back in March. Their locations were south of town, and it was midafternoon. We'd be back to the airport before the infamous Dallas rush hour hit.

When I put my foot on the pedal, I smiled. I hadn't expected the little hybrid to have so much get-up-and-go. We zoomed out of the lot. This was going to be fun. Dallas drivers don't take their time. You have to keep up. At least, that was my excuse for zipping though traffic, but the truth was, I liked speeding things up.

The ride to the first shop, which was the second shop I'd found on Google Maps during my virtual search, took about twenty minutes. This was the one with images that looked like it was a boarded-up warehouse. In person, it looked the same when I drove past the front. I steered the rental to the right at the end of the block and made another immediate right, pulling onto the road behind the building. There I saw what looked like a small store. I slowed, trying to get a peek through the front door window, but the entrance was dark, small, and framed by metal gates. There were two small windows, one on each side of the door, but they were each covered by matching metal bars with no clear visibility. I wanted to go in, but it looked sketchy, and I wasn't one hundred percent sure the shop was even associated with the building on the other side of it, the one I'd seen on Google Maps.

I had attempted to contact this so-called charity back in March. There was no response to the email, and the phone numbers had sent me on a wild-goose chase. I must have found eight to ten different numbers associated with this place. None of them had worked. In addition, I found associated locations, but no one knew anything about the organization. There was one thing this organization had going for it; they were registered with the state as an organization in good standing. I even tried calling the state a couple of times for more information, but I could never get put through to a human.

I went as far as to look up the name that was listed as the registered agent. That was another rabbit hole. It seems about a dozen years earlier, the agent had gotten in some trouble with another charity. The lady had hired her daughter at an above-market rate as a consultant. The couple had also used donated funds for a variety of personal shopping excursions. Yeah, that sounded familiar. None of the information I found proved useful though.

"We're not going in?" Steve asked.

I shook my head. "Not a chance. Nothing about this place feels right."

We got back on the highway and headed south for another fifteen minutes to the second shop, a one-story building that sat back from the main road with a small parking lot that fit only a few cars at a time. This shop seemed more inviting and on the up-and-up, so I told Steve, "Let's get out and see what's inside." I didn't know what I expected to find. It had been months since Esmarelda had donated Mother's things, but I thought maybe I'd find something of hers inside.

When we walked into the store, I immediately veered to the right, where the furniture was on display. I walked in and out of the furniture maze between tables, chairs, end tables, and couches, hoping I'd find something of Mother's. Nothing looked familiar. It seemed like nothing more than a motley collection like you'd find at the garage sales Rachel and I used to go to.

"Can I help you find anything?" the lady behind the counter asked.

"Oh no, I'm just looking around," I said, making little to no eye contact with her. My focus stayed on the clothing racks I'd begun to go through. Again, nothing looked familiar.

I left the store feeling let down, but I wasn't surprised I didn't find anything. I'd already called the shop back in March to inquire about the donated items, and Mitch told me we'd likely not get anything back. Still, I'd held onto some small sliver of hope that maybe something was still there, overlooked and waiting for me to find it and bring it home.

Despite the strained relationship I had had with my mother, I loved her. The last few years of her life, the gap between us widened, and while dementia and physical distance share some of the blame, I put most of it on Esmarelda. I trusted her to put Mother's interests before her own as her caregiver, even when it went against my gut feelings. The years leading up to Mother's death, I'd tamped down my suspicions for myriad reasons. Living so far away, I needed help. I couldn't uproot my life, and Mother didn't want to uproot hers. I struggled with guilt around that decision, especially as more of Esmarelda's deceitfulness had come to light over the last few months.

Being able to find some of Mother's belongings that had been so casually tossed aside during the moves she made during the last few years of her life would've felt like a small victory. Yet, once again, my hopes were dashed. If I could talk to Esmarelda, she'd probably have some excuse that Mother's belongings wouldn't fit in her new place, the one after the Athena. But that would be a lie because I had begun to realize everything that came out of that woman's mouth was meant to manipulate and keep us from discovering her true intentions—to have Mother and her money all to herself.

19

— · —

VICTORIES AND SETBACKS

June/July 2022

By mid-June, we achieved one small victory. Mitch had received notification from the insurance company that they were halting the annuity payout to Esmarelda and redirecting it to an interpleader. This development brought us closer to our family's ultimate goal: consolidating the funds within probate court so that decisions regarding the will and the annuity could be resolved in a single proceeding. I feared that separate handling of these decisions in different cases could lead to conflicting outcomes.

That small win ignited my positivity and sparked an idea. What if I looked up Tracy, the daughter of my mother's former neighbor, Mrs. Johnson, from the Athena? Mother had met Esmarelda one day after she'd "snuck" bagels to her after leaving Mrs. Johnson's condo. It was this meeting that eventually led my mother to hire Esmarelda. I knew how Mother had met Esmarelda, but curiosity about how Tracy had found Esmarelda gnawed at me. I also wanted to know if she had encountered any issues with Esmarelda while working with her.

Locating Tracy wasn't difficult. I'd become quite adept at research and finding people by now, and after finding her on TruthFinder, I called and left a message, unsure if I would ever receive a reply.

About an hour later, my phone rang. The number displayed on the screen surprised me. It was her!

"Hi," Tracy said when I answered. "I'm calling you back about Esmarelda."

"I'm so glad you called. I was hoping I could ask you some questions about Esmarelda's time working with you and your mother."

She didn't mind one bit. She explained her mother had dementia and her ability to care for herself had declined to the point of needing round-the-clock assistance. That's when Tracy found the agency Esmarelda worked for. She did her due diligence, interviewing the agency, and felt confident after speaking with them about their vetting process.

Even though Tracy felt confident the agency hired the best caretakers, she still took some precautions. She lived nearby, so she made it a point to visit her mother every day, always at varying times. As a precaution, she placed her mother's valuables in a safe. Eventually, she also installed cameras in the condo to monitor things when she wasn't around.

For the most part, Esmarelda performed her duties as the agency had described. However, one incident made the hair on Tracy's skin stand up. It occurred during one of her visits to her mother. They needed some household supplies—toilet paper, paper towels—something like that; she couldn't recall the specifics. What she vividly remembered was a credit card on her mother's counter. Esmarelda had reached for the card and offered to go to the store. Tracy took the card from her.

"I told her, 'No thanks, I'll do it myself.' Something about it didn't feel right," Tracy said.

"My mother had told me that Esmarelda was looking for new clients because your mother needed more services and went to live at an assisted living facility. Is that what happened? Did your mother move to an assisted living facility?"

"No," Tracy said. "I just decided to go a different direction with my mother's care."

Ah-ha! That explained why Esmarelda had been canvassing the building for a new client. It wasn't because the neighbor was moving to an assisted living facility. No. She didn't need a new client for a legitimate business venture like she told my Mother. What a joke! Esmarelda was looking for a new mark. Tracy hadn't given her any opportunity to rob her mother's place because she had been monitoring the situation too closely. This was something we hadn't been able to do due to logistical constraints and also because the thought hadn't even occurred to us. We didn't know what we didn't know and blindly trusted Mother's trust in Esmarelda.

I thanked Tracy for her time and willingness to talk. What I thought would be a quick ten-minute conversation had turned into forty-five minutes of discovering that my suspicions of Esmarelda were warranted and our family wasn't alone. Learning that Esmarelda had exhibited similar concerning behaviors early on to what we had experienced felt like another small victory. It reinforced my suspicion that Esmarelda had always viewed my mother as prey. Suddenly, a jolt of energy surged through me. With Tracy's account and the evidence I had begun to gather, perhaps we could finally take our suspicions to the police.

That excitement, however, would be short-lived because in July, a couple of weeks into the month, Mitch dropped a bombshell I never anticipated.

"Esmarelda died ten days ago," Mitch told me.

"She what? No way! I don't believe it."

I truly didn't. Esmarelda dead? It had to be a joke, another con. Esmarelda couldn't be dead. I needed her alive; there were too many unanswered questions: Where's all my mother's stuff? Where's the jewelry? The family photos? What happened during Mother's last few months?

The only question I could ask was, ""What happened?"

"I don't know. Esmarelda's probate attorney contacted me with the news. She didn't provide many details."

I had to restrain myself from blurting out: *Show me the body.* With the annuity payout on hold, suspicions of elder abuse and fraud beginning to surface, and the fact that she had a prior criminal record, I started to wonder: Did she fake her death and disappear?

I knew those suspicions sounded like something out of a Hollywood movie, not real life. Still, truth is stranger than fiction. I wouldn't put it past Esmarelda for a second.

"So, Mitch, what do we do now?"

He sighed. "Well, it complicates things. We need to consider her estate as we proceed with probate."

"Who's representing Esmarelda's probate?"

"Esmarelda's probate attorney."

Esmarelda's probate attorney, Abby Thomas, had originally been hired by Larry to probate Mother's will. I never asked Larry how he'd found Abby, but I know she wasn't on the referral list Curly had given him. Aside from what I saw as an obvious conflict of interest, later on when Mitch received communications from Abby, Mother's name was misspelled. It was spelled how her former doctor, her neighbor and Whole Foods lunch companion, had spelled it. No one but that doctor and people in Esmarelda's family spelled it incorrectly. It might not seem like a big deal, but for me, it was. Could Abby be in cahoots with Esmarelda's children to ensure they got everything they could from my mother for their mother?

"Isn't that a bit of a conflict of interest?" I asked.

"It's definitely something to consider. But, in the meantime, it's easier to negotiate with one party."

I rolled my eyes. They couldn't have rolled further back into my head. Nothing about this process was easy. It was becoming way more complicated than I felt it needed to be. Achieving answers for our family and reclaiming our inheritance, making sure Mother's true intentions were honored, were the most important goals. Not easy. Still, Mitch knew more about the legal process than I did. I had hired him for his experience, after all.

"So, what's next?" I asked.

"I'll get in touch with Abby ASAP to schedule a hearing to plan our next steps."

"What are those?"

"Well, first we request a discovery hearing."

I liked that idea. Finally, Esmarelda's attorney would be compelled to disclose what Esmarelda had obtained from my mother. Maybe we would get closer to some answers.

I hung up with Mitch feeling slightly defeated. Yes, he worked for me and my siblings, but I still wasn't sure he grasped the extent of Esmarelda's exploitation. Deep down, I felt that Mother had been a small part of a larger scheme, just one more person in Esmarelda's long line of victims. While people humored my suspicions, including Rachel and even Wendy, at times, I knew they didn't believe in the depth of the deception as strongly as I did. Yes, they acknowledged that something seemed off between Mother and Esmarelda, but they didn't subscribe to my theory that Esmarelda was involved in a criminal enterprise. No one else was going to invest the time and energy to uncover what really happened between my mother and Esmarelda.

No one except me.

The first thing I needed to determine was whether Esmarelda was actually deceased. I found a website for Texas that claimed to provide death certificates. I called them, hoping to obtain some useful information. The representative informed me that I could submit a request to check if a death certificate file had been created. If there was a file, then there would be a death certificate. I completed and submitted the form but was told that immediate results were not available. I would have to wait a week or so for an answer. Of course, because everything related to Esmarelda was always a waiting game.

So, I turned to Facebook. I found an account for Esmarelda that was not very active, with only a post or two made in the last couple of months. Her daughter, Holly, whom Esmarelda had occasionally used as a fill-in caregiver, had a more active social media account with regular posts throughout most of 2021 and the first half of 2022. However, there was no mention of her mother's death. The last post was on May 15. The only hint of what could have been Esmeralda's death was on her daughter Mia's Facebook page. She had made a post on June 23, 2022, that read "thinking of you" with a link to Esmarelda's Facebook page. I found it odd. Wouldn't you write something more substantial than "thinking of you" if your mother had passed away?

I don't know. Maybe I was grasping at straws, relying on Facebook posts to confirm Esmarelda's death. I knew it wasn't proof of death, nor of deceit. It was a simple Facebook post to which I was attaching my own interpretation.

My obsession with hunting for answers had begun to drive me to the brink of conspiracy land. Something had to give. I could continue expending time and energy searching for elusive proof, or I could allow the probate court to proceed, collect my family's inheritance, and move on. But I knew I couldn't choose the latter. I couldn't let Esmarelda win from beyond the grave.

Still, while waiting for the death certificate information and contemplating my options, Wendy called me one evening and asked, "Would you be interested in trying something out of the box?"

"How out of the box?"

"Have you ever heard of an Akashic Records Reader?"

20

— · —

THE FIRST WITCH

JULY 2022

I absolutely had never heard of an Akashic Records Reader. When Wendy told me she had a friend who worked with one occasionally, I pictured the catacombs of a library and a person sitting at a poorly lit table, poring over dusty old books in dim lighting with their glasses sliding down their nose. I told Wendy as much, and she laughed.

"Not quite," she said. "It's more of a spiritual practice. The belief is that everyone's life has a cosmic record that shows all you've done in your life."

"So, she's like a witch?"

"I guess you could call her that if you want."

"How could she help us?"

"The reading she does can explain relationships and sometimes give you guidance or explain a person's life. Maybe it can unlock some answers about Esmarelda and her relationship with Mother. Fill in the blanks, so to speak."

"You don't think it's a gimmick?"

"My friend recommends her, and her readings are reasonably priced, so I figure it's worth a shot. I actually set up an appointment to speak with the reader next week."

When I told Wendy I'd be willing to try something out of the box, I wasn't expecting something so out of left field—or in the spiritual, psychic realm. Still, we'd been bumping up against one dead lead after another going the conventional route. What could it hurt?

I spoke with Wendy after her reading to find out what the process was like and if it uncovered any new information for us to go on.

"It was definitely different," Wendy told me. "The reading started with a prayer that she said would lead to opening my records, and then it got really interesting. She told me about a house along a lake with a small beachfront. On the beach were two older men, Esmarelda, and Mother. The men had buried Esmarelda up to her nose in the sand. While she was buried, they went in and out of the house bringing out items to Mother, who waited on the beach for them. The reader said they gave Mother jewelry, coins, furniture, and a bunch of lamps."

"Wait. She said all those items? You didn't tell her about those?"

"No. Not at all. But, yeah, I thought the same thing. Why in the world would she mention those items? She also told me one of the men was very angry at Esmarelda and that he had been there for a long time, possibly decades."

"Been where?"

"The beach, I presumed. The reader said the man kept saying, 'They're all going to drop.'"

"Did she give you any clue about what that meant?"

"No, but we talked some more and then she mentioned she also saw Mother on her knees crying, saying she didn't mean it. Then she saw another woman who told Mother to get up and come on. I figured that might have been Mother's mother talking to her."

I'm not going to lie. It was a little weird but not entirely out of my zone of reference. As teenagers, Wendy and I had been exposed to new-age methods and lifestyles. Our dad had lived in Venice Beach in the seventies and had explored alternative experiences, such as walking on hot coals, attending weekend group retreats, and the like. While new-age ideology wasn't something I typically explored, I couldn't stop thinking about the items the reader mentioned. Although not specific, they did match some of Mother's missing items.

Maybe I should give the reader a try too.

The reader's name was Sue. I accessed her online calendar and set up an appointment for an over-the-phone reading the following Saturday.

Before the appointment, I prepared a short list of questions to ask, depending on which direction the conversation went. I wanted to make sure I didn't show my hand. I didn't want to ask leading questions that could be easily answered.

When Saturday arrived and Sue called me, she began the process the same way as Wendy's—with an opening prayer before "opening" my records.

The first thing she told me was that my mother was presenting herself to her as a forty-year-old woman.

"Your mother is saying, 'I know you're trying to help, but I didn't teach you to believe in this stuff. I can't believe you both did this,'" Sue said.

Both? Did she mean Wendy and I and the decision to consult a witch? That sounded like Mother, but it was still a generic response—not something that immediately made me a believer. Most people of Mother's generation wouldn't have invested much time or energy into psychic solutions.

Next, I asked Sue some questions about Esmarelda. I didn't want to influence the reading, but I also wanted to provide some direction for the reading. Hesitantly, I asked her if Esmarelda had taken advantage of other elderly individuals before. How many times had she done it? Did she still have Mother's property? If she did, where was it? I also wanted to know if Esmarelda was still alive.

"She has done this before, abusing older individuals. Your mother and one before her were the first time she involved her family members in the scam, though. She involved three of her four daughters. They also have a storage unit. It's not near where they live, though. It's in the boonies. A neutral space."

"Can you tell where it is?"

She paused a moment before answering, "It's east on the way out of town."

I pulled up a map on my computer.

"Is it before or after the lake?" I asked, forgoing my plan not to offer any prompts.

"It's about five miles back from the split at the lake."

"The split?" I asked, looking at the map.

"Yes, the split, where the road goes north to the man's house."

Whoa! Her words sent a shiver through my body. That's the road to the town where Larry lives. I hadn't mentioned Larry. Was he the man she was referring to?

"The storage unit looks like a parking lot, with multiple levels. It's a dark red or orange. The unit is in her third daughter's name," Sue continued.

Okay, the color detail—that one didn't take a lot to figure out. One of the largest storage companies in the country uses orange as its brand color. However, a quick glance at the map showed a multilevel storage facility right at the split. Maybe she was on to something.

"The storage facility has a couple of stars on it. Also, there are a number of boats and truck rigs in the back. They've had the storage unit for some time, between five and seven years. Also, you know how sometimes when a multilane highway goes into a town and narrows to a regular street through the town but then returns to multiple lanes when the road comes out of the town?"

"Yes," I said.

"Well, it's like that. That's where the storage unit is. I also keep seeing the numbers 3117 and 317."

We continued to talk, our scheduled hour stretching to ninety minutes. It wasn't like she was trying to get more money from me—I paid in advance. She had a lot to say and was generous with her time.

She told me Esmarelda's "little gang" had my mother's stuff along with property from the "prior old man." She said he had engraved his name on the underside of the furniture. She went on to describe more of the furniture: a Victorian-style couch, a dark brown couch, and a metal filing cabinet. I felt the shivers go through me again. The furniture pieces she described were similar to what had been in the Athena condo.

"Esmarelda was never interested in working," she told me.

"Oh yeah?"

"Yes, she'd rather 'take it.' She was very jealous of your mother and wanted to live like her. She kept pearls, some rings, and a masculine ring."

Could the male ring be my grandfather's Shriners ring? I couldn't imagine it being anything other than that ring because it was the only masculine ring I knew of that was part of Mother's property.

Before we ended the reading, she performed a closing prayer and "closed" my book. She gave me her email address and told me to contact her if I had any more questions. I thanked her for her time then hung up.

I didn't know what to think about the reading, but I knew one thing for certain: I was going to start looking for that storage unit.

I sat down at my desk and pulled up Street View on Google Maps, focusing on the east side of Dallas to begin looking for the storage unit. There were several storage facilities but only one along the highway coming out of downtown Garland. Downtown Garland is northeast of Dallas and quite small, probably no more than a couple of miles long. The road out of town went west and then due north, leading to industrial buildings and small, low-rent offices in strip malls.

I followed the road on the map for about a mile and a half when I noticed a storage facility at the corner on the left, an orange Public Storage facility. Could this be the one? Nope. The storage facility was only one level. I kept virtually searching, turning left on the map in the direction of another business on the same side of the street. It appeared to be a much older strip mall with three businesses in it. There was a tall sign in the front of the strip mall facing the street that had business names posted. It also listed the strip mall's address, 317. Okay, that was interesting. I kept moving down the street to the next business then turned and looked across the street. The next business had a number of motorcycles lined up in the driveway. I zoomed in on the entrance and my mouth dropped when I read: Five Star Motorcycles.

To say my mind was blown would be an understatement. Honestly, I didn't even know what to think. I'd basically found every clue Sue had given me. The only thing that didn't match up was storage facility levels. The one I'd found by the motorcycle shop wasn't multilevel like Sue had said, but I felt confident I'd found the correct facility. I wasn't sure what to do with this newfound information. I knew one thing for certain, though: I wasn't going to tell anyone. They'd think I was crazy without proof.

But how could I get that proof? Not sure where to start, I gathered the list of addresses I had for Esmarelda and her three youngest kids. I had quite a few because the whole family seemed to move often. The youngest two had places in Garland, but that wasn't enough proof and could easily be dismissed as coincidental. The first two addresses I put into Google Maps didn't yield the results I'd hoped for. Now, the third address, that was interesting. The Public Storage facility I'd just found was the closest storage facility to that address, about a mile away. Her youngest daughter, Holly, had lived at that address about ten years prior.

My findings, at least to me, were interesting, but what could I do with this information? I couldn't tell Mitch what I had possibly found. I'd already gotten the impression he thought I was a "conspiracy theorist." I decided what I could do was to make sure we worded our discovery list to specifically request information about any storage units holding my mother's personal property. I had already started a cheat sheet of discovery request items, so I added that I wanted pictures from inside each of the storage units they rented. I knew this was a long shot, but I wanted to ensure I didn't leave it out of the discovery.

I decided to spend a little more time researching the area Sue had mentioned, hoping to find some better options. I chipped away at this over the next few days whenever I had some free time. While a couple of storage facilities matched parts of Sue's description, they never quite fit all the other clues.

One place I found in Rockwall, though, had a storage unit that backed up to an office building. Still, the facility itself didn't quite match the description I'd been given. This particular building had two large stars on its front. When I looked up the business name, it turned out to be an organization that ran halfway house services. That was pretty interesting, given that both Esmarelda's daughters have had to use those kinds of services. Could they have been staying at one of these houses at the time?

After a couple of weeks of searching for a location that more accurately matched Sue's description, I emailed Wendy my findings. Like me, she wasn't sure how we could use the information. I had considered making a couple of exploratory calls to some of the places I found, but I worried that if my hunch was right, the person answering the phone might know them and tip them off or clam up, especially if they'd rented there for years. At that point, I decided it had been an interesting experience, but it was time to move on. I couldn't shake the few accurate details she'd mentioned without my prompting, but there was nothing more I could do with that knowledge.

My next task was to focus on the discovery request list. I put that together over a couple of days and sent it to my attorney. He updated the list, rewording the items to be broader in their scope. He told me that once submitted, they'd have thirty days to respond.

21

— · —

DISCOVERY

September/October 2022

The discovery results trickled in, not in one package but in two frustrating installments. The first arrived in late September, and the second batch showed up in late October. Both were a chaotic jumble: credit and bank statements tossed in with email exchanges between Larry and Esmarelda, random time sheets, and even a smattering of medical bills. The sheer lack of organization perplexed me. There was no rhyme or reason to it, just another puzzle of communication to piece together.

The day I received the second batch, Mitch texted me and asked if I could talk. The phone rang within seconds after I told him yes.

"I wanted to let you know that Abby called and said there are a couple of documents in the package that reference visits from Adult Protective Services."

"Why the hell were they involved? Do you know what the issue was?"

"No, not yet. I need to see about getting the records through the court."

"Any idea how long that will take?

"I'll work on a subpoena for the case records, but I have no idea how long that will take."

After we hung up, I mulled over the new information. Why would APS have been checking on Mother? I wondered if someone saw something at the condo building or while they were out between her and Esmarelda. Or, perhaps, someone saw Mother acting strangely, wandering or acting confused, and thought she wasn't being cared for. Waiting for those docs was going to be maddening. So, I did the only thing I could: I turned back to the stack of papers already on my desk, hoping some hidden clue might surface from the chaos I already possessed.

I had two primary goals. The first goal was to search for any glaring signs of crime or mistreatment. My gut told me something was off, and I needed the paper trail to back it up. Second, and just as crucial, I wanted to piece together Esmarelda's entire history with my mother. We'd been living in a vacuum of silence since we were removed as MPOAs back in August of 2019, and I needed to fill in those missing years. The mountain of documents was quite overwhelming, but I was determined to get answers. I decided to approach this as if contesting the will meant going to trial because the more legwork I did now, the cheaper it would be in the long run.

When I wasn't at work, I sat at home going through all the medical statements, test results, bank and credit card statements, time sheets from Esmarelda, and email communications between Esmarelda and Larry with a fine-tooth comb. I couldn't believe all the notes Larry had written on different statements and emails. It almost seemed to me that he expected to be sued for unethical behavior or misappropriation of funds.

Something else that struck me were the emails I read written by Esmarelda and what she said whenever she mentioned me, Wendy, or Eric. It seemed anytime one of us had asked her a question or brought up a concern, she turned around and told Larry about the conversation—and not accurately. She seemed to always make derogatory comments about us, such as how unfriendly we were or how we never talked to our mother.

How could she say that? We spoke to our mother as often as was normal for our relationship up until it seemed Esmarelda took over communications, which seemed to me to happen after Mother's new will was drafted in January 2020. After that, getting ahold of Mother became more difficult.

Larry's responses to Esmarelda's emails were even more bothersome. He seemed to agree with her assessment of us. After reading several emails between the two, it became clear to me that Larry wasn't placating Esmarelda, agreeing for the sake of agreeing. No, he seemed to believe everything she told him.

One email Esmarelda sent Larry was the day after I left in January 2022, the last time I visited Mother before her death. She rambled on and on to Larry about how I'd shown up unannounced, wasn't talking to my mother during the visit, and had gone through all the drawers in my mother's bedroom. She distorted the entire situation.

First, I had called ten days before I visited my mother. I actually called two days in a row, but no one answered my mother's phone. I had also left a message describing my plans for the weekend I intended to visit, that I would arrive late Friday afternoon in Dallas on January 28 and stay until midday on Monday. When I showed up that Friday afternoon, Mother wasn't surprised to see me. I'd even asked her if she knew I was coming and she said yes, I was staying for the weekend. Someone told her that. I assumed it was Esmarelda because she had been monitoring all communications Mother made.

Also, what did Esmarelda know about anything that really happened during my visit? She wasn't even there for more than a few minutes on Saturday when I visited Mother. She never showed up on Sunday. The only other person there that day was the quiet caretaker she'd hired to watch Mother in her place. That caretaker must have told her I'd gone into Mother's room and overheard (or perhaps eavesdropped on) my conversation with Wendy. I assumed she most likely told Esmarelda we were scouring Mother's room for things to take—nowhere near the truth!

I had called Wendy on a video call and walked around the bedroom looking through the closet and dresser drawers to see what was in the apartment and what should've been in storage or in the safe-deposit box at the bank like her expensive jewelry that had seemingly disappeared.

Reading Esmarelda's email to Larry regarding that last visit with Mother, I understood exactly what she was doing. She was planting a seed. She wanted Larry to think we were only after Mother's money. That we didn't care at all about her health or welfare, which was ridiculous. We cared, but we'd gotten frozen out, plain and simple.

As I continued to comb through documents, I found three more tests taken for dementia between 2018 and 2019. I didn't know all the medical terminology, but I did understand the scores. A score of 30 meant no cognitive issues were found. Mother scored in the mid-teens on all three tests. Based on the index, the scores equated to mild-to-moderate dementia. Not good. What made it worse was knowing Esmarelda had attended these doctor appointments with Mother. She knew exactly how bad Mother's dementia had gotten and the direction it was headed but failed to relay any of this to us. At that time, Wendy and I still had MPOA. We could've had more of a say in her medical care had we known about the tests, but it seemed we were purposely kept in the dark either by our mother or Esmarelda or both. I truly believe Esmarelda had convinced Mother to stop sharing her medical issues with us, at least those pertaining to her dementia diagnosis, so she could take advantage of the situation.

Other medical documents I found included paperwork documenting several trips Mother made to the emergency room for falls, including a fractured arm and one when she thought she was having a heart attack. I knew of one of the falls that happened in September of 2019. It had happened when her Athena condo had been being repaired after the flood. Apparently, stacks of floor slats had been spread around the den, and while trying to walk across the room and stepping over the stacks, she slipped and fell. But guess what? We never knew that fall caused her to fracture her arm. What else had been hidden from us?

I started reading other emails sent to us in the discovery documents and came across a note from a physical therapist's office. The email had been addressed to Esmarelda, and the PT had given her details on Mother's visit from the previous day and some suggestions for helping her with at-home exercises. Esmarelda relayed this information to Larry.

But something felt off.

Why was the PT giving medical information directly to Esmarelda? Never once had Esmarelda had MPOA for our mother. Mother also hadn't signed any release of information paperwork to share her medical information with Esmarelda.

I gathered the emails and walked into my wife's home office. "Hey, guess what I found? It looks like one of the PTs emailed mother's medical information to Esmarelda."

"Let me see that." She took the paper from me and gave it a quick once-over. When she looked up from the paper, I saw the concern on her face.

"You know, this is actually two HIPAA violations," she replied.

"What do you mean?"

"One, she isn't on the MPOA, which we knew. But, two, the PT is sending medical information through an unsecure method. Esmarelda's Yahoo account is unsecure."

"Yeah, Yahoo, Gmail, none of those are secure."

As I headed back toward my home office, I made a mental note to talk to Mitch and see what we could do to get into her Yahoo account and look for any other medical information we were never given. Beyond that, I had a feeling that email account could be Esmarelda's Pandora's box. I couldn't wait to open it and see what she'd been up to.

22

— · —

SPREADSHEETS

NOVEMBER 2022

After finishing my first pass through the discovery documents, a pattern began to emerge. Beyond the medical invoices and the endless, irrelevant email chains that read more like a gossip forum, one activity screamed for attention: spending. It wasn't just any spending; this was the kind of financial free-for-all you'd expect from a young couple furnishing their first—or even second—home. And then some.

Esmarelda seemed to always be on a perpetual shopping spree. The sheer volume of transactions baffled me. I mean, how one person could buy so much was beyond my comprehension. The expenditures, using Mother's credit cards, weren't the measured, deliberate financial footprint of an affluent eighty-year-old woman. Not even close. I didn't understand why the bank didn't question the unusual activity on Mother's card or that purchases were made all over town. I was determined to follow the money trail and figure out what Esmarelda had been up to.

First, I reviewed Mother's credit card statements. Activity on her Neiman Marcus card stopped in mid-2019. But her Citi Mastercard activity was a different story. The two Citi cards accounted for 90% of all the spending. I had first asked in March 2022 if I could get online access to the accounts to download the statements, but that request was ignored by Larry. I asked again in late summer. Again, the request was ignored. Larry knew I wasn't up to any funny business like trying to use the cards to go on a shopping spree or pull out cash. My take was he was just being a jerk. So, I had to manually enter all the transactions from her statements into a spreadsheet. It took a few days to do, as I didn't merely put in transaction after transaction with no rhyme or reason. No, I divided the data in the spreadsheet into categories like groceries, household items, etc., so I could sort and filter as needed. I also included the business information and where Mother lived at the time the transactions were made. I knew if I ever had the opportunity to bring this information to trial, having specific information, including dates down to the month, year, and day, would play a pivotal part in the legal process.

As I combed through the credit card statements, I referred back to the credit report I pulled in April. During this time, I noticed Mother's Nordstrom card had some activity on it. Interestingly, that statement wasn't in the discovery documents. I tried to see if I could access it online, using my mother's contact info and her old cell phone. Within a matter of minutes, I had created an online account for the card, logged in, downloaded statements from 2018 and 2019, and had Mother's entire purchase history at my fingertips.

What immediately struck me were purchases that included children's clothing and 2X men's shirts. All of Mother's grandchildren were grown by that time, so what need would she have for children's clothing? Also, Dan had already moved back to Austin by the time the men's clothes were purchased, and even if he had still been with Mother, he didn't wear a size 2X. The only other person who had access to Mother's credit cards was Esmarelda. It was obvious to me who made these purchases.

I finished adding more information to my spreadsheet from Mother's other spending accounts and credit cards and started analyzing her annual spending by year and by month. What I discovered flabbergasted me. You could clearly see when Esmarelda got ahold of the two Citi credit cards in 2018.

Mother wasn't a big daily spender. She didn't need to be. She ate very little and never spent much on food. By 2018, she wasn't going on trips or purchasing a lot of new clothing. Basically, what I surmised her monthly expenses to be were the little food she ate and utility costs. At the end of 2018, the total amount for yearly purchases spent across the two Citi credit cards was $7,000. Not horrible, but by the end of 2019, the total jumped to $53,000. In 2020, the amount climbed even higher, reaching $80,000. In 2021, the total spent across the two credit cards was $60,000.

What was going on?

The first thing I noticed was that between 2019 and 2021, Mother's food bill, which included groceries and restaurants, increased by 50 percent. In 2019, Mother weighed about 100 pounds. By the end of 2021, she was around 90 pounds. I estimated her food bill per week should've been between $75 and $100. But Esmarelda, who by then did all the shopping, was spending anywhere from $400 to $1,500 per month on food between the two cards. She had to be feeding others like her family. There's no way she spent that much on food for Mother and herself, not even for other caregivers she'd occasionally hire to help her care for Mother. Heck, during that time frame, I had a family of four to feed and spent maybe $500 a month on food.

Other large food purchases that boggled my mind were things like $250 from a BBQ restaurant on Thanksgiving in 2020. I Googled the menu of the restaurant, and for that amount, you could've fed twenty people. Then, Christmas of that same year was a $200 charge from Whole Foods. I don't know who was eating all this food, but I can tell you it wasn't my mother. By the time I got done averaging everything out, I figured Esmarelda was spending $800 a month on food.

If that wasn't bad enough, I realized something else as I pored over the statements. For the last nine months of Mother's life, she was living in the assisted living facility, where her monthly rate included three meals a day. By the end of December 2021, Mother was barely eating anything. Yet, if you looked at her grocery bills, you'd call me a liar. Seven out of the nine months Mother was at the assisted living facility, her grocery bill exceeded a thousand dollars. The other three months her grocery costs totaled $2,500.

If seeing how much Mother's food costs had been those last several months of her life were maddening, the next revelation left my head spinning. Mother had everything she needed when it came to home furnishings and decor. On the occasions she needed a new furniture item, she purchased pieces from high-end department stores or expensive furniture boutiques. That changed in 2019, close to when I believe Esmarelda got her hands on Mother's two Citi credit cards. This is when the discount shopping began.

The purchases rotated among Target, Marshalls, Tuesday Morning, and a few other stores. Every seven to ten days, the cards were used, and purchases between $300 and $600 were made. How could the bank not have reached out to Mother to inquire if she made those purchases?

That type of change in spending habits should've led to the accounts being temporarily frozen. When I'd gone through Mother's cell phone, I had noticed she'd gotten some emails declining some charges, but that didn't seem to matter. I imagined Esmarelda shrugging the decline off, pulling out the other card, and going about her shopping. The pace at which she spent Mother's money was mind-blowing—quite impressive actually. I had no clue where any of those purchases went, though. I didn't recall anything new showing up in Mother's places—quite the opposite. As Mother moved from the Athena condo to the Turtle Creek apartment to the assisted living facility, with each move, her belongings seemed to disappear.

The issue with going through credit card statements was I could see the stores and the amounts spent but not what was bought. I discovered that some places, like Office Depot, I could request receipts online. When was the last time you went to an office supply store? The average person, someone who isn't a business owner, might go once a year to buy printer paper or printer ink, maybe some pens or notebooks. Esmarelda was not your average person. She used Mother's credit cards at Office Depot on average three times a month, each transaction totaling $50 or more for the last three years of Mother's life.

It took a day or two before I received the digital receipts. I'd requested receipts from ten different days just to see if there was a pattern. Esmarelda went to several different Office Depots in Dallas County. She bought notebooks, gift bags, ID badges, face masks, and dry erase markers and boards. What was she doing with all this stuff?

I noticed with every purchase she made, she also used her store rewards card. I never found any such reward card in Mother's personal belongings and assumed it was Esmarelda's personal card that she used to rack up reward points while spending my mother's money. I proved that theory when I used Esmarelda's Yahoo email to access the rewards info online.

As I continued combing through the receipts, I came across a purchase made in June 2021 for a $165 purchase. The amount was larger than normal, which is why I'd requested the receipt. The receipt showed a purchase of typeset pages with a revision charge as well as pens, notepads, and five garage sale signs. Wait. Why was Esmarelda buying garage sale signs?

CHARLES E. WALLACE JR.

By that time, Mother had already moved into the assisted living facility. I'd even read a couple of emails in the discovery packages where Esmarelda had told Larry she'd gotten Mother settled into the facility, and she and her helpers (aka her daughters) were moving things into the storage unit, presumably the one Larry had taken me to back in March when I came to Dallas to settle some of Mother's affairs. She also said in those emails that some of Mother's things had been given to a couple of charities. Again, presumably the same charities I'd already tried speaking with.

So what was up with the garage sale signs? I couldn't imagine Mother ever signing off on a garage sale. I went online looking for garage sales in Esmarelda's town via the municipal website and found a page that listed upcoming garage sales. Anyone who wanted to have a garage sale within the city limits had to register with the city. I couldn't look up past garage sales, but the website did have a page to make Freedom of Information Act (FOIA) requests. I'd never needed to make one of these requests before and, honestly, never even thought I could. I thought you had to be a member of the media or have an attorney to make such requests.

The second I knew I could request the information myself, I was on it like a dog on a bone. I promptly filled out all the required info and made the request. I asked for garage sale listings from June through August of 2021 and 2022. I asked for garage sales on file using Esmarelda's address in Desoto, a town south of Dallas.

I knew Esmarelda wouldn't have been alive for the 2022 time frame, but that didn't matter. I was convinced her children were part of Esmarelda's con. If they still had some of Mother's belongings, maybe they had a garage sale to make some money. I wasn't sure what information, if any, would come back, but I'd have to wait at least a week.

While I waited, I continued trying to get receipts from past purchases at various stores. Often, the requests were too old to order receipts from the stores listed on the credit cards. Sometimes, I needed the full credit card number, which I didn't have because Citi never included the full credit card number on a mailed statement in case it was lost in the mail or stolen in transit. As a consumer, I liked that safeguard. As a son, trying to figure out what my mother's caretaker had spent on her client's credit card, it was annoying.

I turned my focus to the last couple of months before Mother passed. Two large meal charges at a restaurant on December 14, 2021, and January 29, 2022, caught my attention. Mother hardly ate those last few months, so why were there charges for meals at a high-end neighborhood restaurant? Each totaled roughly $156. I sent an email to the restaurant and asked if they could provide me with a detailed receipt of what had been ordered. On the December purchase they sent over, there were two $30 meals and four glasses of wine. The receipt noted it was a party of two at 2 p.m. The restaurant's manager had been unable to provide me with the second receipt.

Something about those dates tugged at my memory. What had happened on those days? Wait. December 14. That was the day Mother went on hospice. January 29 was the day I went home from my last visit with Mother.

Oh my God! Were those celebration meals? With Mother going on hospice, was Esmarelda celebrating one step closer to getting her big payday from Mother's will and the annuity?

I started to wonder if Esmarelda had ever used Mother's cards for other "celebrations." I scrolled through the statements again, going back to 2019 and looking for charges for over $100 at a restaurant or bar. On September 19, 2019, I found a charge for $142 and another a few days later on the twenty-third for $202. The nineteenth was the night of what I'd come to call the "Great Toilet Flood." One could argue that Mother and Esmarelda had gone out to eat because they couldn't cook at home.

What I really wanted to know was: Was there a pattern?

I turned my attention away from the restaurant charges and back to the entire financial activity on Mother's accounts. As I sifted through 2021, a series of visits to Home Depot leading up to June immediately caught my eye. There were several purchases of $200 and even one for $300 in late May and on June 1. I tracked down Home Depot's customer service number and called. The representative was very kind but couldn't pull the actual receipts. She could, however, see the transactions. I asked if she could simply do a screen print of these and send them over, which she graciously agreed to do.

Along with those 2021 receipts, I provided her with a couple of dates from early 2020. She located those as well, and what they revealed was telling. On each receipt, perhaps 20 percent of the items could have reasonably been for my mother, but the remaining 80 percent were entirely out of place. In May 2020, Esmarelda purchased an astonishing volume of landscape and planting supplies—enough to outfit an entire house, not a single apartment. She made similar bulk purchases in late May 2021. This time, however, she added a few "goodies": packing boxes, most likely for my mother's upcoming move, along with barbecue supplies: grill cleaner, lighter fluid, rib rub, and more. It certainly sounded like someone was throwing a party. Esmarelda was moving my mother into an assisted living facility, bringing her closer to the will's payout. It looked suspiciously like another celebration meal.

Over the next few days, I continued my search for shopping patterns. Suddenly, an email notification popped up. It was my FOIA request; remarkably, they had turned it around in just a few days. The email contained a link back to the city's website. I logged in, clicked on my document, and the list that appeared almost made me laugh. There were seven listings from June 2021 through June 2022. Five of them directly coincided with days my mother's property was reportedly moved to the storage unit.

My mother moved into the assisted living facility in mid-June 2021, and Esmarelda held two garage sales on the second and third weekends of June. She then hosted additional sales in August and November.

But that wasn't enough.

My mother passed away in March 2022. After looking through her apartment in mid-March, Larry had the remaining property moved to storage on the weekend of April 1. Esmarelda then proceeded to have two weekends of sales in the middle of April. And still, she wasn't done.

After my sister and I had picked up the final few things we wanted to U-Haul back to my place in Illinois in late May, she did it again. The first weekend of June 2022, another sale. Each of these sales had been preceded by a charity donation slip. These slips had vague descriptions like "boxes of sheets" or "shoes." Some even listed furniture, such as "a table and some chairs." The last sheet was my favorite: simply a receipt with the organization's contact information, a date, and a "thank you." After seeing what little had been left in the storage facility when Larry took me in March 2022, I knew without a doubt that Esmarelda was skimming several items before getting the charity receipt.

I looked back at those dates and realized a window of time was missing. Every one of those sales was tied to activity with the storage unit. However, there had been storage activity around January 1, 2022, but no corresponding garage sale. Why not?

I went back to the statements to find that charge.

The U-Haul pickup was in West Dallas on January 1. The storage unit was across town, about twenty minutes away. Yet the statement showed the return was on January 4, in Corsicana, Texas. What?! Corsicana is about 45 minutes south of downtown Dallas. What on earth were they doing down there? And the mileage charged was 460 miles! The actual mileage should have been under 100 miles. How in the world did they manage that?

I'm not sure what their original plan was, but one of Larry's notes from late December 2021 suggested he was fine with all of Mother's belongings going to charity. He claimed we, her children, had told Mother we didn't want to pay for shipping any of the furniture, so it could be given away. The problem was, we never discussed the contents of the boxes. And just how many boxes were there? I wasn't sure, so I had to dive back into the emails. I recalled seeing a check written around that time to Esmarelda's friend but hadn't connected it to any specific work.

Pulling out my file of notes and emails, I eventually found several documents with matching pictures. This woman was truly something else. She'd taken photos of the U-Haul, mostly full of boxes, and her friend's pickup truck, also stacked high with them. Hmm, funny, there was no sign of any furniture. The next document was an email Esmarelda had sent to Larry, proudly declaring they had delivered 120 boxes to multiple charity locations. Then, there was her bill to Larry, again stating 120 boxes were moved and sent to charity.

I pulled out the two charity receipts Larry had given me for that period. Looking closer at the furniture listed, I realized there was no mention of any beds, TVs, a coffee table, or the China cabinet. Since those significant items were missing, I decided to count the boxes on the receipts. Hmm, the math didn't add up. The two receipts combined for a total of seventy-seven boxes. I double-checked the totals. Nope. The billed 120 boxes had inexplicably shrunk to seventy-seven. Maybe they consolidated a few, but certainly not that many.

It was strange. Over the prior five months or so, the more I uncovered, the more I believed Esmarelda planned on living like my mother. She was about the same size, so she could wear those outfits from Chico's and Neiman Marcus; she seemed to have lifted some nice jewelry; and now, it looked like she was furnishing her house with some of my mother's and grandmother's pieces.

When I shared my theory with others, they often looked at me as if I were crazy. But I'd insist I was right about this. For example, with her putting 460 miles on that U-Haul, I believed she was setting up a new life for herself after Mother died. That was far too much effort just to give property to charity. And that town—what was with that? I needed more information.

That weekend, early Saturday morning, I decided to go to our local U-Haul office and see if I could get the actual receipt. I walked in just after they opened, and the place was dead quiet. I approached the counter and found an employee who looked to be under 30 and seemed pretty friendly. Good, I thought. I didn't want to negotiate with someone my own age; they tend to ask too many questions.

I walked up and asked if he could help me. I told him my story, even pulling out the credit card statement to show him the transactions. He took the information and started typing on the computer. There was a chair in front of the counter, so I took a seat. Suddenly, the printer whirred to life. The employee reached over and handed me the first page. He went back, typed in a few more entries, and again the printer started up. He handed me the second page. I quickly scanned each page. Cool! These were the pickup and drop-off receipts. In fact, they had the exact address for the drop-off along with the time of day. I looked up, smiled, thanked him, and quickly headed for the car.

I knew the pickup location, but now I had the drop-off spot. When I got home, I pulled up the map and typed in the address. I was hoping to find some answers with this address, but it only led to more questions. The map navigated me to a spot south of Corsicana. It was barren, perhaps ten miles out of town. All that was there was some little run-down-looking restaurant. This had to be wrong.

I turned on the Street View and looked around. There was a U-Haul truck in the parking lot but no sign anywhere indicating it was a U-Haul shop. I zoomed out on the map to see more of the area and searched for any U-Haul shops in town. Four other locations popped up, spread through the middle of Corsicana. If they were coming from Dallas, they would have driven past all those locations. And since there were no signs out front or on the street indicating this place was a U-Haul facility, they had to know that particular spot.

What were they up to?

I kept staring at the map and realized a major highway ran through town and went straight to Houston. Was she looking to move there?

While I was snooping around, I contacted Wendy to tell her what I had found and what I was investigating. We talked for a while, tossing out suggestions of how they might have traveled around town.

"I've been playing around with different destinations," I told her.

"Maybe she was going to Houston. Let me try it," Wendy suggested.

"I even tried making the trip to San Antonio, since she was from there, but that didn't work," I added.

"Wait, guess what? You can make it to Houston and back to the drop-off spot and hit about 460 miles."

"Well, it's an interesting thought, but there isn't much we can do with it for now," I said, getting a little tired of not finding any real answers. We speculated about a couple of other options, nothing significant. As we hung up, I told her I'd let her know if anything new came up, and you know, something did because there was always a surprise around another corner—always.

23

— • —

CONNECTING THE DOTS

NOVEMBER 2022

With Mother's financial statements thoroughly reviewed, I shifted my focus to the other documents I'd spent so much time organizing into neat piles. My attention had been so consumed by tracking expenditures that I hadn't yet looked through these files. I hoped when I did, something new would jump out at me.

Thumbing through a folder of miscellaneous items, I stumbled upon a copy of a check. To my surprise, it was from Esmarelda to my mother. It took me a moment to grasp its significance, but there, in the memo line, it stated the check was for Esmarelda buying Mother's 2001 Lexus.

What the hell?

I'd thought that car had been traded in for a new one. Then I saw the amount—$2,000. That struck me as incredibly cheap. I quickly checked Edmunds.com for a ballpark value. Mother had used the car sparingly before Esmarelda arrived, so the mileage should have been low. Based on the estimate the website gave, it suggested Esmarelda had paid only half the car's actual value. This discovery gave me an idea.

Having previously leased three cars, I knew that new car paperwork often included a Carfax report. I wondered what my mother's old Lexus Carfax would reveal. I called the sales guy I'd worked with at the Honda dealership where I'd recently bought a car. I asked if he could run a Carfax on Mother's car, providing him with the VIN I'd found on an old car insurance document in the file. I gave him my email address, and he said he'd send it over in a few minutes.

About twenty minutes later, an email from the dealer popped up. I opened the attachment and began reading. It didn't display the owner, so I emailed my sales guy back, asking why. He told me that since the car was registered out of state from his dealership, he couldn't see that information. Another freaking dead end. Oh well, it was a shot. I suspected Esmarelda never registered it or bought insurance for it.

I was curious about the mileage when the car was sold. As I reached the end of the second page of the Carfax report, I saw the last mileage registered on it was just over 80,000 miles. I did some quick math from prior maintenance notes from the Carfax report, which included the current mileage at the time of each maintenance service; Esmarelda, in the two years she had access to the car, before she bought it, was averaging roughly 16,000 miles per year. That's insane. But the most significant entry was next: She bought the car in mid-December 2019, but it didn't last. On May 25, 2020, she was in a wreck. Karma? The note mentioned moderate damage to the front end. There were no more maintenance entries, leading me to suspect it was totaled. That made me laugh—this woman might have been a thief, but she was cheap. There was no way she paid to have it fixed. But I had to know what really happened.

I turned my attention back to my computer and looked up accidents in Texas. The Texas Department of Public Safety website keeps track of accidents where an officer was dispatched. I downloaded the file for 2020. The list was long, but filtering for a 2001 Lexus was quick, taking only a couple of minutes. The report indicated she was driving in Grand Prairie, about twenty minutes west of her house, around seven in the morning. The comment stated she hit a guardrail and smashed the front of the car. The wreck was towed, and the report listed the towing company. Then I saw the driver noted: It wasn't Esmarelda driving; it was Mia, Esmarelda's second daughter. Jeez, they'd only had it for about six months, and her daughter totaled my mother's favorite car. What a waste. Mia was also given a ticket by the local police, which piqued my curiosity even further.

Like most towns now, Grand Prairie has a useful feature allowing you to look up court proceedings for misdemeanors or felonies. Since I had her daughter's full name, I typed it in and quickly found a match. She was fined $360 in May 2020, and as of November 2022, it was still outstanding. There had been a court date for her in August 2020, but it seemed she was a no-show. What a bum! But it didn't surprise me. Her mom had taught her well: Don't spend your own money unless you have to.

The open ticket made me curious about something else. I pulled up the Tarrant County court website, where Grand Prairie is located, then the Dallas County court websites. I then decided to look into the surrounding neighboring counties. I searched each of those with her daughter's full name. This family continued to amaze me. Mia had multiple arrests for unauthorized use of a motor vehicle in multiple counties. Basically, she was a car thief. I noodled around a little more online and found a lovely mug shot of her taken after one of those arrests. Based on the dirt on her face, I guess she lost that race.

With this new information fresh in my mind, I began to connect the dots from one idea to the next. One issue throughout my mother's time with Esmarelda had always puzzled me: the extent of the flood in the condo in September 2019.

The bathroom was at least 10-foot by 10-foot, with the toilet in the back corner. The damage from the overflowing toilet was reportedly so extensive it had reached the adjacent walk-in closet, another closet across the room, and even out the bathroom's entrance, which was diagonally located from the toilet. The volume of water was sufficient to penetrate that opposite side closet wall and flow into the main room, damaging some wood flooring. As a result, the main room's wall had to be replaced, and the flooring, some ten feet out from the wall, had to be pulled and replaced.

My mother had mentioned back in 2018, during my last visit, that there had been issues with toilets backing up in the building. She'd expressed concern that the building was aging, with issues that come with older buildings, but she didn't want to move. I pulled out those insurance pictures I'd found in the bank box and located the ones of the bathroom. Studying them, I concluded there was no way a single flush and backup would have caused that much water overflow. And, even if it did, someone would have thrown down a couple of towels to contain it. That volume of water had to be from multiple flushes. But how would you do it? And why would you do it?

Starting with the how, I decided to call the condo manager. He'd been there for quite a while and was very familiar with my mother and her place. I wanted to get a copy of the maintenance report; I figured there had to be one, as insurance would surely ask for it with that much damage.

It took a couple of calls and messages, but eventually, I reached him. I explained who I was and what I was looking for. He told me that, unfortunately, since the unit had been sold, the documents associated with her condo had been archived off-site. He said he would see if he could locate them, but it might take a few days.

"Let me ask you something. Did any other unit have plumbing issues like my mother's place?" I asked before we hung up.

"No. We had a few units with some toilet backups, but nothing like your mother's." He paused then continued, "You know, we did find something in the pipe that didn't belong there."

"Really, do you recall what it was?"

"I don't offhand. Let me look, and I'll let you know in a few days," he said.

He sounded sincere, so I gave him a few days, which stretched into a week with no response. Not wanting to harass him too much, I gave him some more time. At the same time, I was curious: What could you put in a pipe to stop it up? I looked online, but nothing stood out, so I decided to ask around.

During that time, I'd been playing in a golf simulator league that met one night every week from November to February. The league was structured with two two-hour blocks each night, involving two two-man teams playing nine holes. The guys in my group and those in the second rotation were mostly current and ex-first responders and construction workers. One of the guys in my group did a lot of building maintenance, including repairs and plumbing. The next league night, I decided to approach him with my question: How would you clog a toilet to cause multiple flushes to overflow?

That next Wednesday, I arrived early for league, wanting to chat with him before we started playing. After we had warmed up and sat down at the table, I began to explain my story and what I was looking for. He told me you could buy a stopper, something cheap and easily placed in the toilet and just as easy to retrieve later on. I asked him for the name of the device, which he said was called a test plug or a drain seal.

As soon as I got home, I looked up the stopper. I found it was sold at most hardware stores, including Lowe's and Home Depot. I pulled up the statements from early September 2019. There was a Lowe's transaction about ten days prior to the flood. The same day, there was a transaction at a breakfast place. The amount was more than what my mother would have spent, so I decided to see if I could get copies of those two receipts.

I contacted the breakfast place through their website. The service representative said I would need to contact the franchisee directly. She gave me that information, and I called them. They were very nice and were able to locate the receipt. I gave them my email address, and she sent it over. Next, I needed to find the Lowe's receipt.

I found their contact information and called them. After verifying the transaction dates and store location, the representative was able to find the transaction. Again, I gave the representative my email address, and he sent the receipt. I opened both emails to see if my long-shot hunch was right.

I figured if Esmarelda wanted to further isolate Mother from us, a little plumbing mishap that displaced her would do the trick. It would also give Esmeralda the time she needed to make off with some of her stuff with no one being the wiser. But, to go along with their motive, they likely needed a contact familiar with plumbing. While performing all those internet searches, I had found that the executor for Esmarelda's will was a plumber. Seemed like Esmeralda surrounded her by people who could always help her out.

I clicked open the email from the breakfast restaurant. The receipt showed there had been two customers, and they ordered a couple of normal breakfast dishes. Again, this was too much food for my mother, so I had to assume that the second person wasn't her. The transaction occurred at 11:45 a.m.. Hmm, let's see when the Lowe's transaction occurred. Opening the email, I scrolled down the receipt. It was all cleaning supplies. That's odd. The time on the receipt was 12:30 p.m.

The Lowe's she went to was about five miles north of the restaurant. And then it was another four miles or so back to my mother's place. She could have stopped at the Target in the shopping center across the street. That center was right up the road on the way. Why go out of your way for those supplies? But there was one thing not on the receipt: that toilet plug. So, that was one hunch gone. Now, yes, she could have used her own money to buy something like that, but her recent history showed nothing to suggest she would spend her own money on anything related to my mother's activity. Feeling that I wasn't getting anywhere, I decided to call the condo manager again. It had been a few days, and I couldn't wait any longer.

Amazingly, it only took one call. The front desk guard transferred me to the manager's office. He told me he hadn't been able to locate the archived info, but he did remember what they found. He said it was an adult diaper. It had been stuffed down into the pipe. They also found a small piece of metal, like the tip of a metal coat hanger.

Oh, that was interesting. I knew there had to be something that caused that much damage. So, I was partly right. Now I was stuck with the question of, was that on purpose or not? Based on this information and the outcome, I asked myself: Who benefited?

That flood is what forced my mother out of her beloved condo of over twenty-five years. She never would've willingly left the condo. Based on our previous conversations, Mother made it perfectly clear she had no desire to downsize. She planned to stay in the condo until she died. I'd even found in the discovery documents a letter handwritten by Esmarelda in April 2019, declaring that Mother didn't want to move out of that condo. The letter was signed by my mother. It appeared to have been given to Larry.

So, what changed?

Around the time of the flood, about six weeks earlier, was when Wendy and I had been abruptly removed from the MPOA and replaced by my mother's two friends. The claim was she needed someone local for an emergency, but we knew it was because neither of them would ask any questions. I remember thinking, Well, my mother has Larry and her longtime broker working with her; they should be able to stop any funny business. How naive I was because as I went through more of the documents, I was shocked to discover how wrong I'd been.

24

— • —

DECLINED TRANSACTIONS

APRIL 2023

The first few months of 2023, my focus had split into three areas. I was still trying to find any information online or through receipts that would prove Esmarelda had committed financial elder abuse and block her estate from getting any of my mother's money.

It's how I spent most of my free time.

Because of the probate court's backlog, our initial trial date wasn't until late June. This was actually a benefit. Had this been normal, pre-COVID times, I would have had only a few months to perform all this research. My assumption was that I would take any evidence to a mediation process or trial, if needed. The goal was to work out a settlement and never see a courtroom by presenting any evidence during a mediation process. A trial would only be the last resort.

I didn't really want to see the bill for a trial, but I'll tell you this: I'd gladly pay the $500,000 in fees out of Mother's estate to ensure Esmarelda's estate didn't see a single penny.

The second area of focus was directed at the ongoing legal procedures my attorney was working through. We had the discovery from Larry, but now he was requesting the same from Moe and Curly. In addition, he was trying to get the attorney representing the insurance company to have the annuity funds moved from the federal court over to the probate court. Since we successfully blocked the payout of the annuity, the insurance company had paid the funds to the court through the interpleader process, which had been our goal from the start—to have the funds be part of one decision through probate.

For me, 2022 had been a hell of a year. First, I'd lost my mother. Then, I had to deal with the fallout of Esmarelda's financial deceit. To say I'd been distracted would be accurate and, really, an understatement. Somehow, through it all, I still had what I began to refer to as my day job.

For six years, I'd been a project manager in the Mortgage division of one of the United States' larger banks. Then, at the end of summer in 2022, I'd been encouraged by the bank's HR department to consider looking for a role that was different from what I was used to doing. I decided to follow that advice and ended up in the Customer Experience division, which was divided into four teams that aligned with the four different bank divisions: credit cards, retail, private banking, and mortgage.

The group I was in focused on insight and analysis that help identify drivers of customer dissatisfaction. To put it more simply, we solved problems and tried to prevent them. My technology background aligned with monitoring the bank's digital products, such as the mobile app and the corporate website. While this move brought professional opportunities and growth, it also gave me something else: access to the team that managed the branded credit cards that my mother had been using. Luck seemed to be on my side for once!

In the fall of 2022, I found a source who could help me dive deeper into my mother's transaction activity. Since I had access to her email account through her old cell phone, I'd already known that there'd been a number of declines over the three years Esmarelda had access to the cards, which I found odd. Mother had been what's referred to as an "affluent client." Her credit limit was over $35,000. There should not have been any declined transactions because she should've had the credit—unless someone was using that card suspiciously or had maxed it out.

Mother's email history had told me part of the story regarding the declined transactions but not everything because there were large blocks of dates missing. Mother had used folders in her email account to organize things, but most of that stopped in 2018. After that point, random months of emails were missing from 2019 through 2021. I knew Mother wasn't controlling her devices at that time, so I assumed Esmarelda had deleted the information. My belief was she had deleted all those emails to hide the declined transactions. With so many months of missing information in the email, I assumed there were a lot of declined transactions that had been deleted.

My source had access to the authorization and transaction database tables. All credit card accounts are stored by unique IDs, but having the statements for both accounts, I just gave him a couple of unique transaction amounts to eventually match up the accounts. He then pulled a quick report that covered 2013–2022, focusing on declines.

I wasn't disappointed by what he discovered. But to say I was shocked would be an understatement. For over a decade, Mother's accounts had been open with no declined transactions. Then, once Esmarelda took over the credit cards, the declines ticked upward at an alarming rate. It wasn't one or two transactions that were declined. No, there was an average of twenty, sometimes more, a year. Combine this with the drastic shopping starting in 2019, all the shopping spread throughout Dallas County...well, come on.

Mother's transaction history showed she didn't spend money like that and was completely abnormal for a woman in her seventies with dementia who didn't drive. Of course, the banks only looked at the data; they didn't know Mother's health status, but still: How were Mother's credit card accounts allowed to be left open? The activity screamed potential financial elder abuse. This should have been stopped, but it wasn't. Why?

Getting to the why meant investigating without setting off any bells. My new role might have put me in a better position to gain access to information regarding my Mother's accounts, but I had to be careful. Rules and boundaries regarding personal information still existed—and for good reasons. I was simply searching for evidence that Mother had been a victim of financial elder abuse, but not everyone would see it that way.

I began my research with a contact I had in the fraud unit. His team's work focused on building and monitoring algorithms used for tracking credit card transactions. I emailed him a couple of questions about monitoring and changes in customers' shopping patterns. He replied they already do that. I asked how their monitoring incorporates tracking for elder abuse activity. He told me the company isn't allowed to use age in their monitoring. What? How do you track for elder abuse if you can't use their age?

I couldn't believe it, but it explained some of what had been happening. But just because the bank couldn't identify elder abuse through transactional monitoring, the volume of declined transactions should've been a red flag and set off some type of alert.

A month or so later, I found an opportunity to speak with another source in the fraud unit. During our conversation, I brought up the issue of how confused I was that all this activity on both of my mother's cards didn't set off alarms. That's when I learned something new. It seems that even though you can have more than one credit card account, and both can be seen with a single customer login through their website, the backend monitoring isn't combined. I was told by my second source that, yes, we know it's an issue, but there isn't anything we can do about it at this time.

Brilliant. Glad to hear the bank is truly interested in protecting their customers. So, if a user gets a decline on one card based on activities or location, they can pull out the other card and still make the purchase. That is nuts. People like Esmarelda get away with spending thousands upon thousands of dollars and never getting caught, just inconvenienced when one card declines and they must reach for another. In banking terms, card usage is siloed in relation to fraud monitoring, which automatically decreases the ability or opportunity to investigate a potential abuser.

That's when I decided to take another approach. I figured since the bank wasn't very good at identifying financial elder abuse from transactions alone, I would present my mother's accounts as a case study through my team's review process. I thought at the time that seemed logical. I had asked a couple of the sources who had been with the team for a while if they had heard of any accounts showing up as financial abuse. No one had heard of one. Great, so I approached my manager with my story. I submitted my issue through the review channels.

However, once the issue was assigned to the team aligned with the fraud unit, the movement stopped. I had been watching the activity in our tracking system and noticed that suddenly my issue was closed. I read a little more and found a note stating that there was already a team working to address financial elder abuse, and my situation would be resolved with that solution. Again, it seemed logical.

I asked around and found out the issue was being tracked through a different system—one specifically for fraud and risk monitoring. I had used that system before for another issue, so I was familiar with how to navigate it. Once in, I searched and found a couple of issues being worked on that related to elder abuse. It seemed that Internal Audit had noticed a gap, so the teams were addressing the issue. But upon reading more into the details, I soon realized that this issue was only addressing client interaction, either in person or over the phone. They were going to place the emphasis of reporting any suspicion of abuse on the frontline resources.

This didn't make much sense to me at all. So, essentially, the bank was relying on some of the lowest-paid workers to report potential issues tied to the wealthiest clients at the bank. If they make a mistake, and that client finds out and raises a fuss, guess what is likely to happen? The bank wants to keep that customer, so that low-level employee will likely be looking for a new job.

Feeling dejected at this point, I went back to the supervisor within our group to ask a couple of questions. She had been the one who told me why my issue was closed. I sent her a short email explaining what I had found and my concern that the issue still existed. She wrote back saying that since the account is closed, the next time an abuse case comes through, we can address it then.

I just stared at the screen, dumbfounded. You didn't notice the issue the first time and were only aware of the account because I told you. What makes you think you will notice it the next time? What a wasted opportunity. It's no wonder they are always getting in trouble with regulators—and why elderly and other susceptible people keep falling victim to financial fraud.

25

PROFESSIONAL INCOMPETENCIES

April 2023

Just as I was feeling disappointed and a little angry with how flippant the bank seemed about flagging potential elder financial abuse cases, I received a text message from Mitch. He'd been working to obtain access to the Adult Protective Service (APS) files and finally had some information for me.

Finally!

I couldn't wait to dive into the files and get a better understanding of what had been happening with Mother behind our backs. As eager as I was to get into the files, it also brought out a lot more questions—and unexpected emotions. One of the first pieces of information I read was who they believed had called APS. I wish we had.

Even though it had become more and more obvious that Esmarelda didn't have Mother's best interests at heart, none of us had called APS. Why? Well, because we thought we had to have actual proof of abuse or neglect, not hunches. It wasn't until later we found out we could've reported her just because we believed there was an issue with her relationship with Esmarelda.

So, if we didn't call APS, who did? I thought it might have been a neighbor or a friend. I also figured we might never know because people can make anonymous reports. But it wasn't a neighbor, friend, or an anonymous source.

Esmarelda made a mistake—a big one.

Those large checks my mother and Larry were writing to her? She deposited them into her personal account instead of a business account. I know this because I saw the front and back of the canceled checks. You see, when a personal account regularly has multiple large-dollar check deposits over $10,000, it raises Anti-Money Laundering (AML) flags for the banks' fraud teams.

Supposedly, at some point, Esmarelda had told my mother she wanted to start her own home healthcare agency (or had). I'm still unclear on the details of that conversation. What I do know is that, if Esmarelda had started her own agency and opened a business account, the large deposits wouldn't have raised any suspicions. There wouldn't have been any issues.

But Esmarelda didn't do that because, it's my belief, that was a lie she told mother to boost her credibility. However, Mother's bank where the checks had been written never reported her. I believe the APS investigation is also what drove Esmarelda to open a personal account at the same bank location as my mother. I'm equally sure, but have no proof, that Mother introduced her to a wealth banker, thus providing a cover and turning off the AML monitoring on Esmarelda's account.

Here's the deal with the APS file: I want to tell you more about what was in it. There are some telling bits, including details related to discussions between Mother and the state that clarified more why APS had gotten involved, but I can't because I agreed not to release that information. I can say that circumstances were explained, but ultimately the case was closed following a handwritten letter to the agency from my mother stating Esmarelda would continue to be the lead caregiver for her personal care and the main person in charge of her business dealings. Here is what my mother supposedly wrote to APS, unedited for grammar and punctuation. This letter was in the discovery documents from Larry:

> On May 12, 2020 I recieved a telephone call from APS Jessica Schmidt, caseworker, that the investigation was closed and no further information was necessary. Ms. Jessica Schmidt requested that I inform Ms. Esmarelda Gomez of the decision to close the case was satisfied and she no longer needed to speak to her, I informed Ms. Esmeralda Gomez.

> Ms. Esmerelda Gomez will continue to be the lead caregiver for my personal care. Additionally, I would like to state that Ms. Gomez will continue to coordinate and communicate on my behalf any necessary information needed by Realtor, Betty Arguello, on contract to sell my condo at the Athena 6335 Northwest Hwy, Condo 417 Dallas TX 75225, communicate with Carl Keller, Manager at the Athena when necessary. Ms. Esmarelda Gomez will continue to communicate & coordinate services by Hubb Insurance Flood Loss Claim when necessary. Any additional compensation to Ms. Esmarelda Gomez will be solely at my discretion and Mr. Larry McKibben POA.

There was no way it was written by my mother, a woman in the mid-stages of dementia. In fact, that letter was so professionally written that I doubted Esmarelda had written it, but someone else did. And it wasn't my mother. Yet it was taken as proof that Mother's cognition wasn't questionable and she wasn't being taken advantage of or manipulated—completely the opposite of what was happening.

(I later found that this letter was actually written by the Realtor, Betty, in coordination with Esmarelda. Betty was also bilingual, and they had numerous email threads that were in Spanish. Betty was trying to find Esmarelda a plot of land outside of town.)

The whole file was so frustrating. Elder abuse was sitting right in front of them. They just couldn't see it because they were asking the wrong questions. And doubly frustrating, the agency representative showed up for the first interview days before the new will would be executed. Oh, what a missed opportunity. I bet that scared Esmarelda.

In the end, four banks were involved with this relationship. Two reported bank activity to APS. The other two banks—the one that the two credit cards were drawn against and the other being Mother's longtime bank and the same one Esmarelda began using—made no reports.

But someone had to have suspected something was up. Right? I went back to my emails that contained discovery information. I was looking for a folder that contained some email threads from April 2019, about a month prior to the annuity issuance, and Curly had been talking to Moe about the situation, specifically, the reason for the annuity. Curly mentions something about researching elder abuse.

That's strange, I thought. Why?

The next email thread shows Curly sending questions to one of those Listservs for attorneys:

Client is concerned that if she becomes ill or incapacitated her children will want to move her to a nursing home...Anyone have any experience with which POA would control whether the client was to be moved to a nursing home?

Where was that coming from? A year earlier, I had taken my mother to the assisted living facility where her longtime friend lived. She'd seemed genuinely interested in the place and even put down a refundable deposit, but when we went back to her Athena condo, that's when she got upset about having to get rid of her belongings in order to downsize, and I never spoke to her about moving again. Neither did Wendy to the best of my knowledge.

Why would Curly be researching options to protect my mother from us moving her into a facility a year later? I can only guess this was driven by Esmarelda's grooming.

Fast-forward to November 2019, and Curly is at it again in the Listerv. This was leading to the new will's formation but after the July letter from the neurologist explaining my mother lacked capacity to make medical and financial decisions.

This time, Curly is explicitly asking how to evaluate whether a gift for a caregiver is appropriate. He mentions the CPA, Larry, asking if making a large gift as part of a will might minimize his exposure, but he still questions whether it is proper.

"The fact that you are questioning it is your answer!" I shouted at the screen.

Oh, and that neurologist's letter from back in July? Larry had received it also. Those two men were well aware of my mother's mental state. And to top it off, the email exchanges were six weeks after my mother had to move out of her place due to the flood. She was not in a stable frame of mind—and they knew it.

But it gets better.

Curly received responses from two other attorneys. They provided direction that, if taken, might have had this group of fiduciaries thinking more clearly. He summarized the attorneys' feedback and sent it to Moe:

"I spoke with a couple of elder law litigators about the situation ... Here are their suggestions.

Have the client meet with the client's doctor and confirm the client is mentally capable of making financial decisions. If possible, this should be done within a day or so of the transaction.

Did the caregiver come through an agency? If so, then the agency contract may prohibit such gifts. Or, did the caregiver come knocking, raising possible exploitation?

Do a background check on the caregiver.

They said it's very difficult to determine what is really going on. One mentioned there is a fine line between exploitation and genuine care."

I couldn't find Moe's reply, but two weeks later is when the letter showed up that was written by the doctor Mother knew at her Athena condo—the one she'd occasionally eat lunch with at Whole Foods—that said she was competent. But here was the problem with that document, which I knew now:Hhe could only state an opinion because he was a general practitioner. He wasn't a neurologist, and his opinion lacked any test-based evidence. It didn't prove or disprove anything. It was useless.

That was the same letter that had been typed in all CAPS, with my mother's name misspelled—the same way Esmarelda's daughters had spelled her name. These were the things that fueled my conspiracy theories.

These emails all made me nuts. Curly had suspicions of exploitation, twice. He had gone through the trouble to research the topic and even received some useful guidance. But he still went through with updating the will and having it executed. And then, to seemingly cover his bases, got a letter regarding Mother's mental capacity. Did he ask a neurologist for this letter? Nope. He had Larry, a CPA with no medical knowledge, draft a letter stating her mental competency.

The letter stated that he'd known Joell for twenty-five years, helping her with tax preparation and other tax and financial matters. He writes that for the last year, he's helped her with writing checks to pay her bills and visits her every two weeks to help her with this task. He reviews the bills with her, making sure she understands what she's paying for and how much. With her approval, he then writes and signs the checks.

He then goes on to say in the letter that over the last couple of months, Mother had expressed interest in changing her will. He says the changes have been discussed several times and her wishes have been consistent.

He believes Joell is aware of and understands the provisions of her will.

Well, thank you, Dr. Larry!

How could anyone take this letter at face value? It presents more questions than answers. Why did she need you to write checks for her bills now? What was driving this change in her financial habits? Why did you need to be sure she was aware of what she was paying for? Then, after describing these changes in her ability after twenty-something years, he then states he BELIEVES my mother is aware of and understands. This man had seen her tax returns over the prior twenty-some years. He knew that she had never donated a significant amount of money to anyone outside her family.

You know what I believe? I believe that not only was he going along to continue getting paid by my mother, but that during the drafting of the new will, I found in my Mother's email it was his bright idea to insert the No Contest clause. Why was he concerned about the family contesting the will? The more I read, the more infuriating the situation became.

Then, to top off my day, I decided to check my mother's email account. I was randomly monitoring it in case anything suspicious came in. When I pulled up the account and scrolled back a few days, an entry jumped out. It was a notification from the bank where her brokerage account was held. They had recently declined a transaction from Sam's Club for an annual membership. This was May 2023.

What the hell? The last time that card had been used at Sam's was the week prior to my mother's death. Esmarelda had gone on a $1,000 shopping spree, split between two locations. My mother's membership had been dormant for several years. This was on Esmarelda's account—and by now, Esmarelda was supposedly dead. I contacted Sam's to try and verify what account was using my mother's card. But Sam's can't look up accounts by credit card numbers—at least, their frontline reps can't. The accounts were all associated with cell phones, so I could only assume I was right. All I could wonder was what other surprises could be coming from Esmarelda's past activity.

26

— · —

THE SECOND WITCH

OCTOBER 2023

B y now, I was starting to get frustrated with the pace of the case.
Everything seemed to move at a snail's pace. My attorney was
gradually working to get additional statements from Moe's new organization. Also, the estate now needed to file taxes, which required Larry to
be appointed as a temporary administrator. This meant he had to obtain
a bond for the value of the estate. The premium for this bond would be
an ongoing charge until we reached a settlement and the court completed
an audit of the inventory records.

Trying to stop Esmarelda's estate from getting Mother's money was
costing my siblings and me a fortune. Even if the money wasn't coming
out of our pockets, it might, when all was said and done, if all the funds
in Mother's estate were eaten up by litigation.

I started to feel like progress from research had stalled as well. And
there were just so many odds and ends, things I felt were connected, but
I couldn't prove it. The last couple of months, my attorney had been
negotiating for us to get access to Esmarelda's email account. Gaining
access to Esmarelda's email would be a huge win, but with the possibility
of thousands of emails in the account, we needed to provide specific
search terms to make the task less daunting. I gave Mitch some keywords

that I wanted to search for in Esmarelda's email. He forwarded those to Abby, who said she'd send those accounts to a third-party tech company to produce the results based on the search words. We were given no time frame for this to happen. Who knew how long it would take, but at least there was some light at the end of the tunnel.

I went back into my mother's email account and discovered something interesting. While she was at the Turtle Creek condo, she was getting notices from the post office's Informed Delivery Service about what mail was going to be delivered that day. This service takes a digital image of a person's mail before they receive it, usually a day or two, to let them know what is coming. In one of the email notices in July 2020, it showed an envelope addressed to Joell Flemming, with two Ms, not one, from the Grand Prairie traffic department. It had been forwarded from her original condo address. Interesting. This was the town where Esmarelda's daughter had totaled my mother's Lexus. Also, once again, my mother's name was misspelled.

I quickly pulled up the Grand Prairie court records and searched for her daughter's name. It seems she was ticketed for that accident and fined $350. Better yet, there had been a court date to pay the fine back in August 2020, but as of October 2023, that ticket was still unpaid. I could only surmise that since Esmarelda's family were the only ones to have ever misspelled my mother's name, she gave them my mother's information as the car's owner and insurer. However, Esmarelda's daughter must have filled out the form and misspelled her name. What a family!

This information got me curious, so I went back into the emails Larry had provided. Scrolling through the documents from May 2020, I was able to piece together a timeline around the wreck. The accident occurred on May 25. Then, Esmarelda sent an email to the insurance representative, copying Larry, in which she claimed on May 27 that she was finally able to get the title changed into her name. She told them there had been a backlog due to COVID-19 and that they could now take her off my mother's car insurance. What a bunch of bull-you-know-what! She bought the car in December 2019; the COVID-19 shutdowns didn't start until March 2020. She told them to cancel the insurance because the car was sitting in a junkyard! Just another lie to Larry. How could he continue to be so clueless—or was he? I couldn't figure out if he really believed everything Esmarelda told him, if he played along because he was afraid of being called out for improprieties, or because he was a part of the scheme.

As interesting as that discovery was, I still felt I was missing something. I wanted some help but wasn't sure where to turn. I wanted to speak with Sue, the Akashic Records Reader from last year—as crazy as it was, she seemed to pick out details that no one could have known without our family telling them. Unfortunately, she was nowhere to be found. Wendy had heard she was back online, but none of her sites or links worked.

And then something synchronicitous happened: I ended up speaking with a woman named Marlayna in Nevada who had experienced elder abuse with her parents. I'd met her through a writer's resource group in New York. I'd been writing my mother's story for a while by then, and I was looking for publishing resources. Apparently, her parents' caretaker had been stealing medical supplies. We spoke a couple of times about our experiences, and in the process, I joked about even speaking with a witch. I told her about speaking with the Akashic reader a year earlier and what my experience had been. She laughed and told me she had been using one on and off for several years. She claimed it helped her understand her mother more since she had passed away. Well, that was funny! Could this second witch help me too?

She gave me the woman's contact information, and I got in touch with her, scheduling an appointment a few weeks later. This reader approached the practice slightly differently than the first. The first simply told me yes or no, perhaps including some straightforward descriptions. This woman was more formal; she worked through intermediary beings she called "angels," and she recorded the conversation, providing me with a full transcript afterward. Her method of answering questions was also unique: a single-word response would be spelled using a combination of upper- and lowercase letters, with the strength of the answer indicated by the proportion of capital letters. But, like I did with the first reader, I did my best not to give too much information so as not to lead her. She started off by saying that my suspicions were likely correct about Esmarelda still being alive.

Oh really? I thought. That's interesting. No one else really bought into that theory. It was mine alone.

"Her group paid someone who was already sick to switch identities," she told me. "However, it will be very difficult to prove it. They brought someone in from the north to act like Esmarelda."

"What can I do, or where can I start?" I asked.

"She is part of a group—what you might call a syndicate. It is why she spent so much money on groceries. She was feeding five families."

Wait! What? I never hinted at or told her of the excessive grocery spending. How could she have known that?

"Now, you need to continue your research. They will make a mistake and be lazy. You will find something toward the end of the year," she said. "However, they are selling on sites that don't record transactions. They don't use sites like eBay. Also," she added, "they ditched the U-Haul in January in that town south of your city to throw you off."

She told me they accumulated so many miles on the U-Haul because they were taking my mother's property to different locations east of town. She said that is also where Esmarelda was living now. I asked her what name she was using.

"I am seeing the name Lola," she said but couldn't give me any more details. I did try to get the town Esmarelda was living in now, but she just gave directions to a small town east of ours. That was a dead end as she had no other details that I could use to search for her.

We spoke for a few more minutes. I had been taking notes during the call, but she said she would send a link with the call recorded and a transcript as well. I thought that was a nice touch, as I was sure I had missed a couple of details. I especially wanted to go back over the conversation regarding her claim that Esmarelda's death was fake. How was I going to prove that? Then I had an idea.

Back at my computer, I pulled up the website for Denton County, where her death certificate was issued. I was curious about a couple of things. Again, the hospital was about an hour north of her house. When had she gone to the hospital and how? If she had really been in the ICU, my guess is she should have come in by ambulance. So, I looked up the Fire Department and their contact information. I wanted to find out if there was a way to make a FOIA request for 911 records.

The person who answered the phone was very polite. I asked her what their process was to request or look up 911 records for an ambulance pickup and delivery to that hospital. She directed me to a link on their page to make the request. She told me I needed to provide some personal information, which I had. She said it takes about ten days to get a response. I thanked her and quickly filled out the form and hit submit.

Next, I was curious if the county's Medical Examiner had performed an autopsy because one of the things the second reader told me was there was no autopsy—none had been performed. I scrolled through the site and found the ME's office. I decided to call this time because I was growing tired of emailing and waiting around for responses. Luckily, the office was still open.

"Denton County Medical Examiner's office. How can I help you?" a woman's voice asked in my ear.

"Hi, I was wondering if you could assist me? I wanted to find out what the rules were for when an autopsy is performed," I asked.

"Oh, sure. Of course, we do those when a family makes a request. But otherwise, we will do them if someone dies within 48 hours of being admitted to the hospital."

"I'm trying to see if you may have had one performed on a relative who passed back in June 2022."

"Well, actually, there is a part of the county website where you can look up the names of people who came through."

Great. That would make things easier. I hoped. I thanked her for her time and checked out the county website she gave me. I tried several versions of Esmarelda's name. No luck. There was a date range, so I tried that. Nothing. This meant she must have been at the hospital longer than two days. I was disappointed, but I knew it was a long shot from the start. I'd have to wait for my FOIA response, which was due any day.

An email popped up a few days later from Denton, Texas, Public Information. I opened it to find this: *Your request has been determined to be overly broad and the City of Denton requests you clarify the following....*

Great. I had given a date range, but they wanted the request to include times of day. The note said they left a voicemail message. I listened to the message and, following the directions, updated my request and hit submit. But that wasn't the end of it. Over the next two weeks, I had to go back and forth as I would receive a message saying my request was forwarded to the correct department. Then finally, I received this message: *The City has reviewed its files and has determined there are no responsive documents to your request.*

I was crushed but not totally surprised. Back to looking online for any new clues I could use.

27

— • —

LOST AND FOUND

December 2023 - January 2024

T wo days before Christmas, I found myself online. Not search-ing for last-minute Amazon gifts with overnight shipping. Nope. I was noodling around on the neighborhood social network-ing platform, NextDoor. For the most part, the platform seemed to be just another way to gossip about neighbors, complain about barking dogs, and post endless suspicious activity reports.

The site hadn't appealed to me before I started searching for my mother's belongings. I wanted to get an insider's look at Esmarelda's neighborhood. I'd been wary of using the site with my real name because I didn't want my name popping up. I didn't trust that her family wouldn't see my name and do something. Do what? I don't know. Maybe use something against me that could affect the probate case. That was the most likely scenario, but, if I'm being honest, they made me nervous. I didn't want them seeing me poking around until I was ready to show my hand.

I decided to create a new account using my mother's middle name and email address. I associated this account with the neighborhood where I knew Esmarelda's last residence had been located. I held my breath as I popped Esmarelda's name into the search bar. Her image appeared on the screen, the same photo she'd used on her Facebook profile photos.

I couldn't believe it! What a wonderful early Christmas present. Next, under her profile photo, I read the oddest description.

Please everyone pray for me. I need many prayers to pull me out of this coma I'm in. My name is Esmarelda Gomez. Please. I need many prayers.

The date read June 20, 2022.

Weird, I thought. Others found it odd too. How could you be in a coma and write you were in a coma?

Those comments went unanswered until a couple of months later, when her youngest daughter, Holly, wrote a comment clarifying the situation.

Thank you for all your prayers. Unfortunately, my mother has passed away. I wrote that post, her daughter who has cancer. It's been months now and life is never going to be the same. My mother's generation was the foundation for which I stand and she was my only parent. I'm truly alone now without that warmth or security of a mother. She was amazing. She's gone. Home is gone.

Wow! I shook my head at her theatrical display of grief that felt insincere, a bid for sympathy. Between the poor grammar and the performance, I couldn't wrap my head around that her words were genuine grief. It seemed to me just another act.

I went to this daughter's NextDoor profile. Surprisingly, she didn't post much—maybe an entry a month. As I scrolled back in time through 2022 into 2021, I noticed that when she did post, she had been selling designer goods, things like handbags, shoes, and watches...so many watches. Where did all those watches come from? I found it hard to believe she'd been an avid watch collector. Maybe a watch thief, but not a collector.

None of that merchandise looked familiar to me. I thought maybe one pair of shoes could've been my mother's, but I wasn't certain. I kept scrolling until I hit September 2021, two months after my mother moved into the assisted living facility and her property supposedly had been put into storage. That's when I struck gold!

I couldn't believe what I was seeing on the screen. Mother's black china cabinet, her antique tea set, a set of silver goblets, a floor vase that I knew came from my grandmother's extra bedroom, and several other items that were definitely my mother's—in Esmarelda's house. I also noticed she had listed a leather recliner for sale. The recliner hadn't been Mother's. However, in the background, I spied a side of the cabinet I 100 percent recognized: Mother's old buffet cabinet she'd had since I was in middle school.

How many things from Mother's condo were in Esmarelda's house?

I went to my storage tub of papers, dropped down to my knees, and pulled out the photos I'd taken from the safe deposit box. My heart beat so fast as I flipped through quickly and found photos matching every single one of those items for sale. I scanned the photos into my computer, then cut and pasted those pictures from Esmarelda's daughter's account into a Microsoft Word document and added the website address. After that, I started a PowerPoint document, building three slides with side-by-side photos. I couldn't wait to send this information to Mitch. I couldn't wait to send it to Wendy and Eric. Finally, I had proof. Definitive proof that Esmarelda had kept Mother's things just like I said. She hadn't put them in storage. She took them home.

The elation of finding Mother's things and getting the proof I'd tried getting for so long eventually turned to anger. Why did Esmarelda think she could take what wasn't hers? Maybe Mother had given her the things. Maybe she hadn't. What I do know is that Esmarelda manipulated the situation to get what she wanted. She'd taken advantage of my mother and that made me furious—and she was no longer around. She'd gotten away with it.

I wanted to send the email with the attached file of my proof to Mitch right away, but I waited until the day after Christmas. I had no idea what his schedule was like that week, but with Christmas falling on a Monday that year, I figured he'd see it by the end of the week. I didn't hear from him, though. Then, my family got the flu over New Year's. So, I didn't reach out until a couple of days into 2024.

"Hey," I said excitedly when I called him. "Did you see my email?"

"When did you send it?"

"The day after Christmas."

"The day after Christmas?! You thought I'd see it then?" He chuckled.

"Well, no. I figured by now you would've. I sent you evidence that Esmarelda's family was selling my mother's property online back in 2021."

"Okay, let me pull it up now." I waited while he found the file. "This is good stuff, Chip. Really good. Let me work on putting together an updated filing. How much did you say the missing jewelry appraised for?"

I gave him a rundown of the missing items and their value, which I believed totaled over $85,000 in missing jewelry. A significant portion of this total, a watch valued at $35,000, was listed on my mother's homeowner's insurance at the Athena. While it was my strong suspicion that Esmarelda had stolen it, I had no photograph of the watch and was relying on a hunch, as my mother had kept it in an unlocked safe. To account for this uncertainty, we decided to request $50,000 in payment to cover the total loss.

"I will put this together over the next couple of days and send you a draft," he assured me.

Finally, I thought. I couldn't believe it took a year and a half to get to that point.

Within a week or so, the final version was submitted to the court and a copy sent to Abby. Oh, I would have loved to have been in the room when they read the new filing. Then a week later, out of curiosity, I logged into the NextDoor account and pulled up the daughter's site.

But wait, it wasn't there. I tried again with no luck. Did Esmarelda's daughter delete her NextDoor profile?

I had an idea. I went back to Esmarelda's account and scrolled down through the comments on that original thread. There it was. She had changed the spelling of her name by using just her first initial with her last name.

I clicked her new name and found myself back on the site I'd remembered. Since she had changed her name, I wondered what else might have changed. I scrolled down her thread, quickly getting to the September 2021 entry. I thought the posts for the china cabinet and recliner would be there. They weren't. She had deleted both entries.

I had to laugh. What an idiot! Did she honestly think I hadn't already copied all the content before reporting back to my attorney? Why did she delete the entries? Was it because she was guilty? It made me wonder about all the other items she was selling, like that box of watches and shoes. If I could, I would have loved to wander through that house, but I knew that was never going to happen.

28

YOU'VE GOT MAIL

MAY 2024

My attorney and I had been working for a year to gain access to Esmarelda's email account. We had heard a number of excuses from the family—primarily that no one in the house had access to it. I never believed this claim. In fact, in the summer of 2023, I received some photos from a man named Darryl, a plumber, who claimed to be the executor of Esmarelda's will. The photos came from Esmarelda's phone. He couldn't simply open the email app on the phone and give me the information?

After months of haggling, the probate attorney, Abby, offered a compromise: They would give the account information to a third party, who could then download emails based on a list of keywords we provided. I agreed and spent a couple of days building a comprehensive list of names and phrases, knowing some would be discarded as "fishing." I organized the terms into four categories to avoid duplication and to rank them, should I need to reduce my request.

A week later, I received an email from Mitch with a link to the filtered emails. I downloaded the file and started reading. It contained three folders, each representing a different date range, from 2017 to late 2023.

Initially, I found little of interest—just a massive amount of junk mail from shopping sites and car auctions. A lot of CVS ads were addressed to my mother, Joell, which was strange. It appeared Esmarelda had signed my mother up for a rewards account but had the emails sent to her own address. It reminded me of the Office Depot receipts I'd come across in November of 2022 that included rewards info. What other services had Esmarelda signed my mother up for? I decided to see if I could access my mother's CVS account. It was surprisingly easy to do using the forgotten password link. I simply had a new password sent to Mother's old email address.

Getting the password proved to be the only easy part. The actual CVS website was confusing as I tried to locate shopping history and receipts. I couldn't find the receipts, but I did find a list of prior purchases, with a link to repurchase the items. I guess it was better than nothing. As I scrolled through the list, I was both shocked and vindicated. It seemed most of the purchases were for Esmarelda. The list included fake eyelashes, makeup in colors my mother never wore, and other items that were clearly not for her, like baby formula. I wondered what else she had been buying under my mother's name.

While the CVS information proved interesting (and my suspicions of Esmarelda), something was off with the data I'd received. It was missing many emails related to my most obvious search terms. I called Mitch to ask about the files, and that's when he told me he'd never given my list to Abby. An oversight on his part, he admitted. He asked me to resend it, and he would send it to her right away.

A couple of days later, my family and I left for a cruise. I took my laptop with me in case the emails from the original list came through while I was out in the middle of the ocean. Boy, was I glad I did. About three days into the trip, Mitch emailed me. He asked if I could trim my keyword search list—considerably. He needed me to get it from 150 keywords to about 20. Since I'd had the list already categorized, that was easy. I pulled the top five keywords from each of the four groups, sent it back to him, and waited.

An email from Mitch showed up about two weeks later with the subject line, "GOMEZ - 2024_0627 PRODUCTION," and a single word: Enjoy. The email contained a Dropbox link. The first batch of emails had perhaps 500 items; this file had close to 6,000. I clicked the link and found six generically labeled folders. A quick scan confirmed there were nearly 6,000 documents. This was going to be fun.

I had several reasons for wanting to access Esmarelda's email account, but the main one was my belief that Esmarelda had a pattern of financially abusing the elderly. The bizarre details surrounding the obituary of Bob Barnhill—the elderly man she had previously cared for—suggested something was amiss.

I opened the first folder and discovered documents dating back to 2009. I had assumed I would only get items from the time she began working for my mother in 2017. The first few items were junk mail, but then I hit pay dirt.

There was an email written to a placement agency that had fired her in January 2009. She complained that they had "unjustly" terminated her on a Friday night. The agency claimed she had inappropriately used a client's—Mr. Barnhill's—personal data. In the letter, she acknowledged being on probation for "mishandling sensitive client documents" in a prior incident but then blamed the organization for offering "no compliance training" and "lacking internal controls." Her accusations had a tone similar to an HR document, and I later found out that Esmarelda's oldest daughter works in HR. It's my belief she guided the writing of that letter.

At the end of her tirade, she dropped a bombshell.

"Let this serve as formal notice that Bob Barnhill and I have a personal relationship that resides beyond the scope of my professional life and he is willing and more than able to provide his rendition to both your Board of Directors and the Adult Protective Services, and we are looking forward to it."

I read the last paragraph again and realized what she wrote wasn't a defense; it was a threat. She wasn't just claiming a relationship; she was using it as a weapon against the people who had hired her. The words "personal relationship" weren't a sign of affection but an admission of manipulation. She was telling them, in no uncertain terms, that she had compromised this man's judgment and would use his trust to get what she wanted. It was a chilling foreshadowing of how she would later work her way into my mother's life and leverage her vulnerability against us.

I couldn't believe it. The organization fires her for inappropriate behavior with a client, which she tries to deny, and then she brags about the inappropriate behavior in the same letter. What a winner!

I had suspected she was a serial financial abuser, but I never thought I would find proof in writing. In a single email, I had confirmation that she was reported to APS while providing round-the-clock care for an elderly man. She admitted to having more than a professional relationship with him and was caught twice mishandling sensitive client data.

But this email was more than just proof of a single incident. It was a blueprint. I saw the same strategy she would later use on my mother, laid bare almost a decade earlier. The pattern was unmistakable.

She first targeted the vulnerable. Mr. Barnhill was elderly and living alone, just like my mother. She then quickly ingratiated herself, moving from a professional role to a "personal" one, gaining access and control over his finances. With him, she leveraged that supposed relationship as a defense. With my mother, she used a narrative of love and devotion as the justification for a will and annuity. And in both cases, when faced with opposition, she tried to discredit us. She had called her agency "unjust" for firing her, just as she later painted me and my siblings as selfish children who didn't care about our mother. It was the same playbook, repeated with horrifying precision.

Most people would be deterred following such an incident, but not Esmarelda. A couple of documents later, I found she was working directly for Mr. Barnhill. Then in March 2009, she asked his attorney, Kathryn, to add her to his credit card and checking accounts. While not mentioned in these emails, I recalled a POA document filed in January 2011, the month Esmarelda married Barnhill. I had always assumed the POA was executed at that time. Out of curiosity, I pulled the document and discovered I was wrong. Esmarelda had obtained the POA in March 2009—two months after being fired for inappropriate behavior! She had control over that elderly man for two years before they married.

The marriage proved very beneficial to Esmarelda. When he passed away in April 2011, she inherited the house, its contents, and $200,000 from his brokerage account. Based on Esmarelda's previous ten years of moving from apartment to apartment, this was the nicest home she had ever acquired. But, alas, she and her family only stayed in the home for four years.

I had seen in the original private investigator report that Esmarelda had gotten into trouble for not paying her taxes. Based on the way she had spent my mother's money, I assumed when she moved from the nice house to a much smaller home in a lower-income neighborhood, it was because she couldn't pay the property taxes. Of course, I pulled the property history from the county records. The documents showed that the new owners in 2016 paid the back taxes for the years 2012–2016.

If there's one thing you need to know about Esmarelda it's that she's nothing if not consistent.

As I continued through the next few documents, I found a letter from July 2009 between Esmarelda and her daughter Mia. It seems they had an argument, and Mia was going to move out of town but needed to return to Mr. Barnhill's home to retrieve her suitcase and clothes.

This reminded me of the obituary Esmarelda had written, which referenced her daughters helping out. It had never crossed my mind that her daughters had moved into Mr. Barnhill's home.

I continued sifting through the emails, but I couldn't go fast enough. Every folder was another gem. There was no way Esmarelda or her attorney ever thought someone else would get access to this email account.

The folders had been organized by year, and the contents jumped around some as I moved from 2009 into 2019. Around April 2019, I started seeing emails with notices for my mother. They ranged from doctor and car service appointments to bank announcements. Esmarelda had set up all of my mother's digital communications to go to her email address. In fact, when I later tried to reset my mother's password on the bank's mobile app, the recovery email was still Esmarelda's.

Unbelievable.

These bank notices were especially of interest to me because they were from one of the two banks that didn't call APS—the ones that had those large personal checks being deposited into a personal account. Activity bank personnel are trained to watch for money laundering. Seeing those bank announcements frustrated me. They could send information about financial products, but unusual financial activity on customers' accounts wasn't a priority.

Another interesting find in Esmarelda's emails were emails from the insurance adjuster who had handled the flood at the Athena. I had never seen any notices regarding the flood in Mother's email accounts and wondered why. Now I knew why. Every bit of communication had gone to Esmarelda's email, including the full insurance adjuster's report, with photos of the damage in the Athena condo. Neither my siblings nor I had ever seen this document, and after seeing the photos, what I always suspected had proven true. The damage wasn't enough to warrant my mother needing to move out and into the Turtle Creek condo. She could have stayed there with assistance until she needed to move to the assisted living facility. She had been persuaded to move.

But that wasn't all that occurred in 2019. When my mother moved out in November, someone arranged for a couple of storage units to be used down the road from the Athena. A peculiar thing happened around that time. About a year or so earlier, I found an online comment associated with this same storage company. However, the comment was for a location they had on the south side of town, about ten minutes from Esmarelda's house. The comment was from Esmarelda on December 21, 2019: "Great friendly professional associate Brantley. She is great and sweet attitude. Thank you." She gave her 5 stars.

I had assumed this meant she was not taking all of my mother's things to her storage place but was instead skimming property and taking it to this other location. But I had no evidence of the storage units until now! The email bills listed each unit and were addressed to her for this southern location. Since my mother moved to a place that was half the size of the Athena, she was never going to see all her stuff again anyway, so there was no way she would know what might have been missing.

Speaking of moving, as I dug deeper into the files, I came across some documents from November 2021. There, between all the junk email, was a signed contract for a house located in a small town I had never heard of. As I was reading through the contract, I realized the real estate agent, Kathryn, was Bob Barnhill's former attorney and his POA before Esmarelda assumed the role. She was the person Esmarelda asked to add her to Barnhill's credit card and checking accounts. And now, according to the sales contract in the email, she was selling Esmarelda a house, which was 60 miles south of town. Esmarelda was a good con artist. Maybe not the smartest, but she knew it was important to keep her fiduciary relationships close to avoid suspicion.

According to the contract, the sale was to be completed by July 24, 2022, but Esmarelda could start moving property into the home immediately. I guess she figured my mother would be gone by then and she'd have the money she needed from the annuity and the will to complete the purchase. I had never heard of the town, so I pulled up a map. The town of Stratman was located about an hour south of Esmarelda's home, in a secluded and rural area. Can you say "stash house"?

The interesting thing about this location was that you had to drive through the town of Corsicana to get to it. This meant you went right past the location where Esmarelda dropped off my mother's U-Haul back on January 4, 2022. This also explained a CVS receipt in Esmarelda's email file from that town, dated May 2022. The charge had shown up on my mother's CVS rewards number transactions, two months after my mother's passing! Did she not own anything in her own name? At that point, I realized she was still receiving all my mother's email communications, from car dealers to doctors to retail stores, even now.

Curious about the house, I pulled up the county records for Stratman to see if I could find the current owner. The tax records showed that Kathryn actually still owned the property. I guess she held onto it since the sale to Esmarelda died with her. I wondered if Esmarelda had actually ever moved any belongings into it and, if she did, if the family ever went back and retrieved the property. I wanted so badly to call Kathryn and ask her all those questions, but I didn't. I didn't feel comfortable doing that until the judge signed the probate papers, whenever that would be.

Maybe I could go out there? I entertained the thought for a moment, but the place was too far out there for me to make a trip just to look around. I contacted the private investigation group we had used before instead. I asked them to drive by and see if they could get a look inside. A couple of weeks passed, but they finally contacted me. They said the property was all overgrown and didn't look lived-in. There was a fence around the property, so they weren't able to get up close to the house. They ended up talking to a neighbor, who said he didn't even realize there was a home on that land.

Then there were two emails that just added to the peculiar circumstances surrounding Esmarelda's death. I had initially searched all the social media sites I could find related to Esmarelda and her family around the time of her death. Her daughters had stopped making entries on her social accounts by mid-May 2022.

I found one email from June 15, 2022, a week before her death. The email from Esmarelda's account was sent to her daughter Holly with an attachment. It read: Joell's will. Why was she sharing the will with her daughter? My mother's will had a provision that any beneficiary had to survive ninety days post my mother's death. That date would have been June 6. Why was she sending the will out now? I can tell you what I believe.

On the 15th, Esmarelda learned we had successfully contested the annuity payout. The insurance company was going to send the contract to a court to follow the interpleader process. She had no way of knowing when that decision would be made. This was a problem for her. That annuity was outside of probate, and she was expecting to receive that $250,000. Now she had to be wondering what information we had given the insurance company to create questions about who should receive that payout. And were we going to the police to report her? Seven days later, she was supposedly dead of an anoxic brain injury.

To add to the curious situation, there was a related email on July 22, 2022. This one had both my mother's and Esmarelda's wills along with my mother's death certificate. The email was sent to an unknown Gmail account that was never mentioned again in any other documents I received. Why were these documents sent out, and who received them? I have searched using multiple search engines and found no sign of that specific account.

On top of this odd situation, I found an email from August 1, 2022, that contained documents required to start utilities at the Stratman house. The document was being sent from Esmarelda's email to Holly's email. I decided to double-check the county records in Stratman to verify who owned the house. But as I mentioned already, Kathryn was still the owner of the house.

Another interesting email conversation was a document thread from early July 2022, in which Holly was begging Larry if any money could be released. Amazingly, he told her no. This was the polar opposite for Larry, who throughout probate had continued to misappropriate funds from Mother's estate—like he did when she was alive, if you ask me. Even though he wasn't supposed to pay bills from the estate until any eventual settlement, he had continued to pay Abby, his legal counsel to the probate, with estate funds.

I wanted there to be a logical reason for all these curious email findings, but over the years, I learned that nothing makes sense with Esmarelda. The only thing that might make sense is something so shocking and illogical that I hesitate to say it out loud.

Esmarelda might actually have faked her death.

29

—·—

QUESTIONS

JULY 2024

While I reviewed email after email, Mitch began working with a forensic psychiatrist. He'd been speaking with her off and on over the previous four months, attempting to get all of my mother's medical records to her. This task proved more challenging than either he or I had anticipated, since one of the hospitals had changed names and one of Mother's doctors had retired. Retrieving all the pertinent doctor visits was necessary because we wanted to make sure Mother hadn't had any unknown medical visits that could contradict the records we had.

Once we had all the information the forensic psychiatrist needed, it would take about three weeks to get the report. While we waited, we continued digging into more background data. Truly, it seemed never-ending, but we had to determine our next steps as we got closer to the probate hearing. Barring no continuations, the hearing would happen in late September of 2024. But to be honest, I really had no interest in going to trial. Don't get me wrong...I would have loved for Larry and Esmarelda's family to be deposed. I had a long and pointed list of questions for Larry, especially as a direct result of all my digging. I couldn't help but wonder how much he'd squirm on the stand if I (or rather, Mitch) ever got to ask them.

For instance, I wanted to know about the missing jewelry. I could imagine Mitch standing in front of him asking, "Tell me the story of the jewelry appraisal. How was that initiated, and what was the outcome? How did you ensure the complete collection was returned to Joell?" My calculations showed that over a quarter of the collection was missing, with a value of more than $50,000.

Then, in my imagination, Mitch would move on to the storage-unit debacle. "In December 2021, just two weeks after Joell was put on hospice, what led you to agree to have the storage units emptied? Why did you assume that when you were told by Esmarelda that the kids didn't want the remaining furniture because they didn't want to pay for the delivery costs of the furniture that it also meant they didn't want any of the 120 boxes? The kids were never even asked about those boxes, which contained priceless family heirlooms: college annuals, childhood photos, slides, pictures, and 8mm film of their youth. What was the reason you never contacted any of the kids to ask about handling the boxes? Why didn't you just leave the storage unit as it was since she was already in hospice?"

I imagined Larry flustered and unable to form a clear answer on the stand because he knew he'd had plenty of opportunity to ask those questions. Wendy had been talking to Larry in December regarding Mother's health and her going into hospice. That would've been the perfect time to do so, but he chose not to.

The U-Haul bill was another gaping hole in the story of Mother's missing belongings. "What was the explanation Esmarelda gave you when you asked her about the January 4, 2022, U-Haul bill that showed 460 miles driven? The mileage should have been between 75 and 100 miles to make around-town deliveries and drop off items to the two charities. What did Esmarelda say when you asked her why they dropped the U-Haul off south of Corsicana?" This location was a good hour south of where Esmarelda lived and where the charity receipts were from.

The financial discrepancies were just as infuriating. "On March 9, 2022, a package arrived the day after Joell passed from Buck and Buck. Esmarelda told you she would return this delivery, valued at $330 and charged to the brokerage account. On what month's statement was that credit applied? What did you do when you saw that there was never a credit applied?"

That's a question I really wanted Larry to answer. My review of all statements from March 2022 to June 2022 showed there was no credit. Then there were the charges from Sam's Club on March 3 and 4, 2022, totaling over $900. At the time, all of my mother's meals were covered by The Preston. When we were in the apartment on March 13, there was not $900 worth of items in the apartment that could have come from Sam's Club. What did Esmarelda say was purchased with these two transactions when you saw them on the March brokerage statement?

The lies about the caregivers were another point of contention. I wanted Mitch to drill Larry on this point. I wanted to know what Esmarelda said when Larry discovered she was billing for two caregivers, 24/7, starting in January 2022, but she only had one caregiver on for many of those days? I know this to be true because I was in the apartment on the last weekend of January. Remember? There was only one caregiver there for those three days, yet she billed for two caregivers, 24/7. The one caregiver told me that when they needed help, they were to call the building staff and an attendant would come and help. The help usually lasted 15 to 20 minutes. Why didn't Larry know this too? Or did he decide to look the other way?

Finally, there was Larry's professional negligence that needed addressing. I wanted to know what his response was when he saw the maintenance report for the flooded bathroom at the Athena. How could he think something didn't add up? An overflowing toilet couldn't have made such a mess. And, last, I wanted to know when Curly asked him and Moe to write a note stating Joell's capacity for signing the new will, why Larry didn't suggest that Curly talk to her neurologist? I knew that Curly's request was because he'd been questioning Mother's capacity.

All of these questions were building a mountain of evidence that Larry had failed in his fiduciary duty. I could only hope he'd be asked to answer for it all—someday.

PART THREE

RESULTS

30

— · —

VINDICATION

AUGUST 2024

C ome August, the conversation between the attorneys turned toward talks of settlement. It was also around this time that a forensic psychiatrist's report made it into Mitch's hands. He'd hired Dr. Loudon to provide a medical evaluation on Mother's mental state earlier in the year to determine if she'd been of sound mind to make the decisions she made regarding her will and the annuity assignment. She did this by reviewing Mother's medical records and evaluating her test scores. Dr. Loudon came highly regarded and was a person known in the legal community as someone competent and fair who regularly evaluated individuals for attorneys in Dallas County for mental-health–related issues for more than a decade.

When Dr. Loudon's report landed in my inbox, to say I was shocked is an understatement. I'd mentioned before that I didn't understand how dementia actually showed up in a person's life. My rudimentary knowledge of the disease had me believing it really was nothing more than memory loss. Even as Mother's illness progressed and I witnessed her become frailer and less communicative, I still didn't fully grasp the severity of the disease. I didn't realize that even in early 2019 that her mental capacity had diminished so much that she'd become overly susceptible to persuasion.

Dr. Loudon had written that "due to her significant cognitive impairment," Mother couldn't have had the contractual capacity when she was alleged to have executed the document naming Esmarelda as the beneficiary of her Nationwide annuity. She went on to note that:

On 01/24/2020, Ms. Fleming had continued to have worsening cognitive impairment, and she would not have had the testamentary capacity to have executed a Last Will...during these times she would have been highly susceptible to undue influence by others.

In Dr. Loudon's professional opinion, Mother's symptoms, based on the medical records she reviewed, had started nearly nine years prior to her death. There were notes in the records indicating my mother had self-reported memory issues back in 2013. Did I notice these memory issues? Probably. I also probably wrote them off as being typical responses from a person getting older. I feel most of her memory deficits she probably hid well until her husband, Dan, moved to Austin in 2017 to live nearer to his children and deal with his own dementia.

It was following their separation that her cognitive impairment became more evident. That is when she began to have problems managing her finances, basic activities of daily living, and self-care. Late summer of 2018 is when Wendy asked Larry to help our mother with paying bills and monitoring the accounts to watch for any funny business, like other people writing checks other than him or Mother. That failed. Larry wasn't the best watchdog.

Dr. Loudon also noted that based on Mother's test scores from October 2018 and February 2019, she was in:

Late-moderate to early-severe stages of a Multi-Factorial Dementia, and she did not have the contractual ability or testamentary capacity to execute any legal document.

There you have it.

Mother's illness created the perfect opportunity for Esmarelda to take over everything in my mother's life. She became the puppet master, the one pulling the strings. She knew exactly what was going on with Mother's mental capacity. It explains why my mother, quite suddenly in April 2019, asked Moe to set up an annuity for Esmarelda. Mother had never given away her money to anyone outside of the immediate family, especially such a large sum of money. Shoot, she rarely gave much money at all, even to her favorite charities. Mother kept her money close, which is why it never made sense to me when she started giving Esmarelda so much.

Another part of Dr. Loudon's report addressed Dr. Brimley's letter from November 2019. Remember him? The general practitioner who lived at the Athena and was my Mother's Whole Foods lunch buddy? I always had suspicions about the letter he'd written regarding Mother's mental state for the new will. It was the one written in all caps and had my mother's last name misspelled in it. Dr. Loudon's findings reported that Dr. Brimley had done no objective cognitive testing at the time, supporting my theory that he had no neurological testing capacity because he was only a general practitioner. However, the documentation from the two neurologist office visits clearly showed a decline in cognitive ability, as the letter from Dr. Jacobson at UT Southwestern's Neurologist office in late July 2019 outlined.

This letter had been given to all three of my mother's fiduciaries. Significantly, Dr. Jacobson never actually met my mother; his professional assessment was based solely on the comprehensive medical records, eliminating any chance for him to have been persuaded or manipulated. My attorney, Mitch, confirmed the weight of this finding. With over twenty years of practicing probate law in Dallas, Mitch had crossed paths with Dr. Jacobson before and knew he had a solid reputation for "going by the book" and medical record history. Mitch stressed that Dr. Jacobson didn't easily issue letters like that unless the impairment is absolutely genuine.

This letter was the one that ultimately led to us being removed from the MPOA in early August 2019. It confirmed what we were experiencing, even if we didn't have all the details. We later learned that Wendy, my sister, had contacted that UT Southwestern office in July 2019 to ask for a letter of competency, hoping to prove Mother was not capable of making competent decisions and bring to light the signs Mother's fiduciaries were ignoring.

The truth was, Mother was secretive all her life, especially about any issue that showed she was aging. I knew about the appointment in October 2018, but none of the other subsequent doctor's visits were ever passed on to us. Even after attending the October 2018 appointment, I never knew the full outcome, other than she was being referred to another doctor at UT Southwestern. Part of that referral was to see a psychiatrist for depression, and we learned much later that she had been prescribed medication in December 2019, which she quickly stopped taking. The only difference after we were removed from the MPOA was that we were unable to legally get information from any of her doctors, but as far as her actually telling us her status, she was never telling us before or after being pulled from the MPOA.

Basically, we learned of all the details, the full history of her mental and physical decline—all the doctor visits, the meds, and the referrals—only after legal discovery began in October 2022. This long silence and the blackout on her health records made it easy for Esmarelda to operate without challenge.

Then, seemingly out of the blue in March 2021, Dr. Brimley's notes opined she had Parkinson's disease and "Advanced Dementia." Dr. Loudon, in her report made a point to note that:

As it is a medical impossible without a catastrophic event, a patient with Parkinson's disease to go from early to advanced dementia between the date of his letter in 11/2019 and his medical diagnosis of her on 5/02/2021 (approximately 18 months.)

This put the use of the second doctor note from Dr. Brimley to rest. It was meaningless since this diagnosis was made well after the new will went into effect in 2020.

So, what did all this mean? What were the next steps? Well, Mitch needed to present the report to Abby for her to find her own expert witness. By this time, we were late into August 2024, with a court date now scheduled for mid-October. And, like I mentioned earlier, talks between Mitch and I had turned toward a possible settlement offer. I didn't want a court bill and knew I had to make a choice quickly because if we weren't going to settle, we needed to start prepping for trial. We discussed numbers, and after a couple of rounds with Larry's attorney, we came to a resolution. We agreed to allow Esmarelda's family to receive the annuity fund but requested to have the $300,000 that had been in Mother's second will revoked. We knew the second will was bogus, but since it had already gone through all the procedural steps, it allowed us to complete probate and stop paying the attorney fees—ours and Larry's—the one thing we wanted at that point more than anything else.

31

—·—

A KIND OF RESOLUTION

SEPTEMBER 2025

T he journey to a final resolution had been a long, slow crawl. At times, I never thought we'd get to the end of the journey. There were times I felt certain the process would go on for so long that my daughters would inherit the case because I'd be long dead myself. Of course, I exaggerate. I knew we'd get to the end of the road eventually, and after three years and some-odd months, we did.

The final delays were less about the complexity of the law and more about the infuriating and slow-moving nature of bureaucracy. The courts were painfully slow, a combination of years of understaffing compounded by the pandemic. I'd heard theories that the courts were deliberately allowing the backlog to grow, hoping to force the creation of an additional probate court to ease the load. Who knows what the truth is. All I know for sure is that the process tested my patience, especially when the most absurd roadblocks caused the case to come to a screeching halt. Like when the probate judge apparently disappeared on a three-week honeymoon without notifying her staff. That's just one absurd example of many I dealt with trying to settle my mother's estate.

One of the most pleasant surprises of the audit of the temporary administrator's activity, which was Larry, was the court caught his typically sloppy reporting and forced him to fix his mistakes. It never should have been this difficult. Had the people Mother had trusted to look out for her done their jobs and opened their eyes to Esmarelda's sneaky, deceitful ways, none of this would've taken as long as it did. Thankfully, once the mistakes were fixed and submitted, Abby, Larry's attorney, filed the final request to close the temporary administrator role.

The court signed off on the final paperwork on Thursday, September 25, 2025. With the final request signed, the money from Mother's estate could finally start being dispersed to us.

Esmarelda's family had already received their money months before. The settlement we had agreed to—ceding the annuity funds to them—had been processed and paid out long before the remainder of the estate could be wrapped up. It was a bitter pill to swallow, knowing their windfall was secured while we waited for the final, *honest* accounting.

My lawyer, Mitch, was also finally due his payment. He hadn't received a penny beyond my original retainer deposit, having worked on contingency for the bulk of the case. Abby, on the other hand, had been paid all along, a fact that made my blood boil. Larry—the fiduciary who was supposed to be a neutral watchdog—had continued to pay Abby's mounting legal bills with estate funds, a practice that was explicitly against the rules while the estate was still being contested. He always seemed to find a way to pay the women who asked. It was his signature move, the one he never corrected, and it perfectly summarized his role: ineffective at protecting Mother but reliably compliant with those who demanded payment.

The case is officially closed now. It's an end but not a resolution. Not for me.

Yes, the money will eventually land in our accounts and will represent the final, measurable outcome of a three-year fight that cost a fortune in legal fees, but we never should've had to fight so hard for what was stolen from us and rightfully ours.

The victory feels hollow. We stopped Esmarelda's final grasp at Mother's wealth, but we couldn't stop her initial theft, nor could we change the fact that her estate still walked away with a significant sum. We managed to expose some of the deceit, the professional incompetence, and the shocking lack of accountability in the systems meant to protect the vulnerable. We proved that my mother was a victim of undue influence.

The court is satisfied. The case is filed away. But for me, the questions remain, forever suspended between fact and devastating conjecture. The paper trail ends here, but the memory of the betrayal—and the image of a cunning predator who may have simply vanished—will never fully close.

And then there's the one lingering thought I can't let go of: Esmarelda might have faked her death.

32

— · —

DID ESMERALDA FAKE HER DEATH?

Comedian Groucho Marx once said, "Time flies like an arrow." Well, he must've never participated in a probate court audit because time nearly stood still. For nearly a year, the case continued to drag on. At some point, I surrendered to the slowness, convinced settling Mother's estate, now three years after her death, might never happen.

While I waited for closure, I spent my time thinking about all the questions I had that never resolved themselves. The main one being Esmarelda's "death" and its timing.

Do I really think Esmarelda faked her death? That's a lofty accusation. Why would someone do that? Aren't mobsters and people like Marcus Schrenker, the American businessman who attempted to fake his death in an airplane crash to avoid paying back millions in investor debt, ones who go to such great lengths? To put their families through unnecessary pain and suffering? That is, if they're not a part of it. I'm not so sure Esmarelda's family are innocent if she did in fact fake her death.

Mitch thinks I'm nuts when I tell him my suspicions. He's never bought me a Christmas present, but I'm pretty sure if he did it would be a tin foil hat. My conspiracy theories always leave him shaking his head, and I get it. He's an attorney. He deals in facts and concrete evidence. And what evidence do I have that Esmarelda's alive?

Let's start with the dubious timeline. The pieces never fit. From the moment I heard about Esmarelda's death, a series of coincidences and unexplained details began to pile up, all pointing to the same unsettling conclusion: she faked her death.

On the surface, her dying seemed like a convenient way to end our legal battle for the annuity and contesting the new will. But if you looked closer, read between the lines of the story we were being told about Esmarelda's death, the narrative began to unravel.

And the unraveling began long before Esmarelda supposedly died. September 12, 2021, to be exact. On that day, Esmarelda left my mother's apartment and drove to Medical City, a hospital that was forty minutes out of her way. I know this because she emailed Larry the next day claiming to have been sick. Why she needed to tell Larry this, I don't know. I also don't know why she chose to go to that Medical City when there was another one just ten minutes away. It's an odd detail and maybe you could write it off, explain it as something as simple as a matter of physician preference. Perhaps she felt the care was better there. Maybe she checked online emergency room waiting times and that one had a lesser wait time. But as I dug deeper, it seemed to foreshadow the beginnings of a plan.

Later, in November 2021, Esmarelda began moving her belongings into the home she was under contract to buy from her late husband's attorney, Kathryn, a whole eight months before the July 24, 2022, closing date. I've bought several homes throughout my lifetime, and not one of those transactions gave me the go-ahead to move anything into the property until monies were wired, keys exchanged, and the deal inked. Now, you might think that's strange too, but stranger things can happen. Right? She knew Kathryn. This wasn't a stranger-to-stranger sale. Maybe it was a special arrangement.

But things became less coincidental and more premeditated when I learned Esmarelda had executed her own will in January 2022. And the attorney who handled the case was Kathryn. I'm not saying the attorney was involved in Esmarelda's elaborate scheme, merely that from what I knew of Esmarelda, once she had you charmed, she kept you by her side for when she needed you.

You might also argue that maybe Esmarelda, having cared for elderly clients, had seen how fast death can come. Maybe, you might say, she decided it was time to get her affairs in order. She was already in her early seventies. She wasn't going to live forever. You might say that, and it would be a reasonable thought. It certainly wouldn't earn you a tin hat, but I didn't buy it.

Fast-forward to June 15, 2022. I succeeded in stopping the annuity payment to Esmarelda. The next day, Esmarelda emailed copies of her will and my mother's will to her daughter. One week later, on June 22, she "died" at a hospital an hour north of her home—exactly 106 days after my mother's death. The timing of Esmarelda's death seemed more than a coincidence: It seemed to me a legal maneuver. You see, my mother's will contained a survival clause. It stated that any beneficiary had to outlive her by at least ninety days.

I found Esmarelda's death itself shrouded in more bizarre details. First, I could never find a published obituary—a rarity, although when I contacted a local funeral home, they told me it happens about ten percent of the time.

Another thing I found odd was the swiftness of her supposed cremation. How convenient for her to have been cremated, eliminating any possibility of an exhumation and further investigation. Then, in early 2024, when I couldn't shake the feeling that maybe the person who'd been cremated wasn't Esmarelda, I made a bold call. I reached out to the crematorium to ask about whether they weighed bodies before they were cremated. If the crematory operators were surprised by my question, they didn't let it show in their voices. They said that, yes, they did weigh bodies before cremation. I asked if I could get information about Esmarelda's weight at the time of her cremation. They told me the body weighed 200 pounds. Now, I hadn't seen Esmarelda since I visited Mother in January of 2022, but I'll tell you this: She seemed to hover between 125 and 130 pounds. Did I weigh her or ask her weight? Of course not. But no way did she appear 200 pounds to me. So, how did she gain nearly 70 pounds before she died? I suppose it's possible she'd gained weight between then and when she supposedly died, but what if she didn't? Couldn't the weight difference raise the question: Did the body at the crematory even belong to Esmarelda?

Oh, and the oddities continued even after the cremation. On July 22, 2022, Esmarelda's will, my mother's will, and the death certificate were emailed from Esmarelda's account to a mysterious Gmail account whose initials matched Esmarelda's and her boyfriend, Gordo's. The Gmail account never appeared again in the thousands of messages I reviewed. I even tried running searches through internet browsers hoping to hit on the email, but I got nothing.

A week later, on August 1, 2022, documents to turn on utilities at that rural home of Kathryn's were emailed from her account to her daughter's.

So, does all this really prove that Esmarelda faked her death—and, more importantly, why would she do that?

Even though she'd somehow manipulated a contestment clause into my mother's final will, I still believe she anticipated that my siblings and I wouldn't let her get away with the $300,000 from our mother's estate. However, she fully expected to receive the annuity payout. After all, wasn't that separate from the will? She was the beneficiary, after all.

Esmarelda underestimated us though. She never thought we could (or would) get the annuity payout halted through the interpleader process. When we did that, we threw a wrench into her plans. Her relationship with my mother would suddenly become scrutinized. She'd be under a microscope. She must've worried more was at stake than the annuity. If fraud could be proven, criminal charges might follow. Of course, Esmarelda wouldn't have wanted to go to jail.

Being "dead" could solve two problems for her. First, it would render any potential crimes uncovered irrelevant. At the time of Esmarelda's death, I hadn't yet discovered her daughter had been selling my mother's belongings online. I didn't realize she'd been using my mother's credit cards for her personal shopping sprees. Those discoveries came later, but Esmarelda knew what she'd done. She knew that she couldn't hide if an investigation was opened.

I believe she also believed being "dead" would solve the annuity payout issue. You see, one of Esmarelda's daughters was listed as the contingent beneficiary. Even as I write these words, it boggles my mind how much Mother had been manipulated. Never would my mother, in her right mind with all her faculties, ever have given away her money like that. Never.

Was my mother a willful woman who cared more about herself than her kids most of the time? I'd argue she was.

Was she someone who enjoyed being lavished with praise? Most definitely.

Did we have a strained relationship at times? That's true as well.

Still, all those things didn't take away the fact that Mother believed in the transfer of generational wealth. She wanted her children to have what belonged to them. She wanted her money and her belongings to stay in the family.

She never would've let a stranger strip her of those things, which were the basicness of her identity.

But that's the thing about dementia. It robs you of what fundamentally makes you, YOU. It clouds judgment. It opens the door for ill-intentioned people to come into your life.

What breaks my heart most about the whole situation isn't the money or belongings stolen. No. It's knowing that Mother believed Esmarelda and her family loved her and were looking out for her. When all along, they were plotting against her, taking whatever they could from her. I'm not sure I've made sense of how that makes me feel yet. Even though every new discovery of deceit should leave me numb and the years since Mother's death stacking up behind me, I still don't know if I should feel angry, mad, outraged, or anything and everything all at once.

But back to the second advantage of being "dead."

I believe Esmarelda figured dying would help her get around all the legal hurdles she felt certain to be in her future. According to the terms of the annuity, the beneficiary had to outlive the annuity's owner by at least 90 days. By the time of Esmarelda's death, she'd outlived Mother by 106 days. However, a payout hadn't occurred yet because I had filed an injunction to stop the payout and move it to the interpleader process. So, what happens to the annuity payout if both the owner and beneficiary die before the payout occurs? You might assume, as I believe Esmarelda did, that it goes to the contingent beneficiary, which in this case was one of her daughters.

That's not quite how it works, though. You see, if the beneficiary dies after the owner dies and the payout hasn't occurred, the money goes to the beneficiary's estate. In this case, the payout wouldn't have transferred to the daughter but to Esmarelda's estate, making it subject to probate.

Such irony!

It's my opinion that Esmarelda faked her death thinking she'd avoid legal scrutiny and still live somewhat high on the hog with Mother's money because her daughter would receive the funds and give them to her mother. I believe that's why Esmarelda had sent those emails that contained her will and Mother's will to that mysterious Gmail account.

But what do they say about plans? "The best laid schemes of mice and men go oft awry," as Robert Burns wrote in his 1785 poem "To a Mouse."

Now, Esmarelda was dead, real or not, and no one had any money. Everything was in probate.

That's very well explained, Chip, you might say. But let's address the other elephant in the room. How did Esmarelda fake her death? The real world isn't like the movies. She died in a hospital. That's kind of hard to fake. After all, there are procedures to follow to make sure when a person is dead, it's really them.

I'll give you that it sounds crazy to imagine someone who's not a mafia boss or hedge fund guy with access to unlimited funds and resources could pull something like that off. It does seem a little irrational, but sometimes the most ordinary people do the most outlandish things when their money or freedom are at stake—and Esmarelda wasn't exactly without access to funds. Over the three years she worked for my mother, she received at least $900,000 for her services. None of that included the money she saved on items like money and clothing that she paid for using Mother's credit cards or the money she saved on transportation once she got ahold of Mother's Lexus. Oh, and let's not forget the over $85,000 in missing jewelry that I fully believe Esmarelda stole. In addition to my mother's money, I also believe she had money from other victims, but I have no way of proving that.

My point is this: She had the resources to fake her death.

So, how did she do it?

223

I believe she or someone close to her, like her boyfriend or one of her daughters, knew someone who was already sick near Esmarelda's age and resembled her enough for no one to question anything. On their deathbed, with very little time left, they decided to seize upon an opportunity. Working for a caregiving service, it wouldn't have been hard for her to find someone in this state. I find it highly probable that Esmarelda then went out of her way to befriend the family of the sick woman and waited. She waited for the woman to be admitted to the hospital, with little to no chance of leaving except on a gurney to the morgue, and then she swapped identities, paying the family to go along with the deception. Esmarelda likely chose someone with a history of blood clots or coronary issues as her death certificate listed coronary artery disease and anoxic brain injury as the cause of death.

I get it. It sounds outlandish. A little too made-for-TV. It's a reach, but something feels off and so I'm reaching...reaching for answers and hoping my fingertips touch something that's tangible and makes sense. That tangible something is evidence, and all the evidence I've collected feels like it's pointing to only one conclusion.

[1] Esmarelda's still alive.

---

1. *County records show Esmarelda's executor came back and bought that little house south of town in early 2025. Remote location, basically off the grid. Hmmm.*

PROTECTING OUR ELDERS

PREVENTING AND RECOGNIZING ABUSE

A fter witnessing the elder abuse of my mother at the hands of someone she trusted, I've become passionate about helping others avoid similar situations. Aging is vulnerable enough. No one should be exploited by someone they entrust with their care. Unfortunately, it happens every day.

According to the National Center on Elder Abuse, 13 percent of elder abuse incidents reported involved nonfamily caregivers. However, I believe that number is much higher, mostly because elder abuse is sneaky. It's not always in your face. It works in the shadows.

So, what can you do to protect your loved one from falling victim to these predators?

What follows are practical tips I've put together from my personal experience with a predatory caregiver to help your loved one experience dignified aging not marred by exploitation.

Tip #1: Safeguard Your Loved One's Finances

Financial exploitation is one of the most common forms of elder abuse and, often, the most damaging because it happens slowly. Rarely does a caregiver take control of an elderly person's finances overnight. It starts small like using their credit card for gas or lunch. Over time, the purchases and the financial abuse grow larger. The first line of defense in protecting your loved one from financial abuse is to protect financial documents by having bank and credit card statements forwarded directly to you or by establishing online access to all accounts, allowing you to monitor transactions regularly. It's also a good idea to set up transaction alerts on all your loved one's accounts so you immediately get notified of unusual activity, withdrawals, or attempted transactions that were declined. I only wish I had seen all the declined transactions Esmarelda had triggered when she'd been using Mother's cards. It would've have given me the proof I needed much earlier to show a pattern of financial abuse and attempt to stop it.

Request monthly reports from the bank regarding any declined transactions, noting the date, location, and amount of each attempt, and inform the caregiver that you receive these reports. Understanding your bank's fraud detection protocol is crucial, as many institutions have gaps in their monitoring systems that could leave elderly clients vulnerable, such as not factoring age into their fraud detection algorithms or treating multiple cards separately even when held by members of the same household.

For day-to-day expenses, provide caregivers with gift cards or prepaid credit cards that have specific spending limits rather than giving them access to your loved one's personal credit cards. Clearly communicate that you expect receipts for all purchases and that you'll be maintaining a detailed accounting of expenditures. This accountability often deters those with exploitive intentions.

Tip #2: Vet Caregivers Thoroughly

Always be the person who hires the caregiver. Don't let your loved one make this decision if you can help it. In my mother's case, she specifically hired Esmarelda, which created an unwritten contract between them. Esmarelda felt like she didn't have to answer to anyone other than Mother, regardless of her mental state, and because we didn't have power of attorney, she didn't have to. From the get-go, establish a system where you, not the person who needs the caregiving, hire and fire any help. This creates a clear power dynamic where the caregiver answers to you rather than controlling access to your loved one.

Selecting trustworthy caregivers requires thorough investigation beyond basic references. Never hire someone based solely on personal recommendations. Instead, conduct comprehensive background checks using resources like county court records, which often maintain separate databases for different types of cases: one for criminal matters like misdemeanors and felonies, and another for civil matters such as marriage filings or power of attorney registrations. Verify professional credentials through appropriate licensing boards and check for any complaints or disciplinary actions. I also suggest contacting the Financial Industry Regulatory Authority (FINRA) through their BrokerCheck service to verify if any financial professionals who may have access to your loved one's accounts have ever had any violations.

Conduct personal interviews with caregivers you're considering hiring. Ask them to tell you how they would handle real-life scenarios to get a better idea of their problem-solving skills, patience levels, and ethical boundaries. Pay attention not just to what they say but how they react to questions about handling frustration, respecting privacy, and managing financial matters. Ask for multiple references and actually contact them with specific questions about reliability, honesty, and how the caregiver handled challenging situations. Trust your instincts during this process; if something feels wrong despite good credentials, it's worth exploring those concerns further before entrusting someone with your vulnerable loved one's care.

Tip # 3: Create Safe Spaces

The physical environment plays a crucial role in both preventing abuse and enabling monitoring when necessary. Make random visits to your loved one's residence at various times of the day to observe interactions, living conditions, and any changes in the home environment. Consider installing visible and hidden cameras with sound recording capabilities in common areas. This isn't to take anyone's privacy away but to deter potential abuse and to document concerning behavior. I recommend letting potential caregivers know from the start that video surveillance is used in the home. Another great way to create a safe space is to make sure your loved one has access to private communication methods that caregivers can't monitor or control, such as a personal cell phone with emergency contacts programmed for quick access.

Secure valuable items in a safe, safe-deposit box, or other locked storage that only trusted family members can access. Create an inventory of these items with photographs and descriptions, updating it regularly to quickly identify if anything goes missing. Arrange the living space to accommodate regular family visits and social interactions, reducing isolation, which is a significant risk factor for abuse. Establish a protocol for regular health checkups with doctors who know to look for signs of neglect or physical abuse, ensuring these appointments happen without the caregiver present for at least part of the visit to allow for private disclosure of any concerns.

Tip #4: Build a Support Network

One person can't completely protect against elder abuse—it requires a team, especially when you're thousands of miles away from your loved one. Use resources like the ianacare app to build a comprehensive support team that includes healthcare assistance, legal references, and access to other valuable resources for elderly care. Assign different family members or trusted friends specific monitoring roles, such as reviewing financial statements, attending medical appointments, or making regular social visits. Establish relationships with your loved one's neighbors who can alert you to unusual visitors, activities, or signs of neglect they might notice during their regular routines. Create shared Google documents where everyone can communicate easily if there are concerns or obstacles.

Maintain open communication with your loved one's bank personnel, healthcare providers, and any social services they interact with, making them aware that you're actively involved in your loved one's care and protection. Remember that Adult Protective Services can investigate based on suspicions alone—you don't need concrete evidence to report concerns, though the effectiveness depends greatly on the assigned caseworker's approach. Create a communication schedule with family members to ensure information about your loved one's condition and care is regularly shared and any concerns are promptly addressed. Regular family meetings, even virtually, can help coordinate care efforts and ensure everyone remains vigilant against potential signs of abuse.

When to Intervene

Recognizing warning signs is crucial for early intervention before abuse escalates. Watch for unexplained withdrawals from bank accounts, new "best friends" who seem overly interested in your loved one's finances, or sudden changes in banking practices such as additional names on accounts.

Be alert to physical indicators like unexplained bruises, weight loss, poor hygiene, or untreated medical conditions that could signal neglect or physical abuse. Changes in your loved one's demeanor when certain caregivers are present—becoming withdrawn, anxious, or fearful—warrant immediate attention and a private conversation with your loved one.

Question explanations that don't make sense or stories that change when retold by caregivers. Notice if your loved one is suddenly unable to access their mail, phone, or transportation, indicating potential isolation tactics by abusers. Be particularly concerned if caregivers refuse to leave you alone with your loved one or answer questions directed at the elder for them.

If you observe any of these warning signs, document them carefully with dates and specific details to establish patterns that might be useful for Adult Protective Services or law enforcement. Remember that reporting time frames vary by state. Misdemeanors, more minor crimes such as a caretaker stealing a nominal amount of money from their client, typically have a two-year reporting window from discovery, while felonies, such as causing severe bodily harm or stealing thousands of dollars from a client, often allow three years.

What to Do When You Suspect Abuse

If you suspect elder abuse is occurring, swift and decisive action is essential to prevent further harm. Contact Adult Protective Services immediately with your concerns, understanding that while they can investigate based on suspicion alone, the quality of the investigation may vary depending on the assigned caseworker. Document all interactions with authorities, including names, dates, and summaries of conversations to maintain a clear record of your reporting efforts. Remove your loved one from the situation temporarily if possible while the investigation proceeds, even if this means bringing them to your home or arranging for respite care elsewhere.

Consult with an elder law attorney who specializes in abuse cases to understand your legal options and the best way to protect your loved one's interests going forward. If financial exploitation has occurred, immediately secure all accounts by changing passwords, requesting new cards, and potentially freezing credit to prevent further damage. Report suspected criminal behavior to law enforcement, providing them with your documented evidence and timeline of suspicious activities. Remember that your advocacy is crucial. Be persistent with authorities if you feel your concerns aren't being adequately addressed, and consider reaching out to local elected officials or elder advocacy organizations if you encounter institutional resistance to your reports of suspected abuse.

The journey of protecting our elders from abuse requires vigilance, compassion, and practical knowledge. By implementing these strategies—financial safeguards, thorough vetting, physical monitoring, support networks, recognizing warning signs, and taking decisive action—we can create a safer world for our aging loved ones. Remember that prevention is always preferable to intervention after abuse has occurred. Your attentiveness today could spare your family the heartache that mine experienced and ensure that your loved ones age with the dignity and respect they deserve.

Protecting Our Elders Resource List

- Adult Protective Services (APS): https://www.napsa-now.org /help-in-your-area/

- U.S. Department of Justice: Elder Justice Initiative (EJI): http s://www.justice.gov/elderjustice/

- National Center on Elder Abuse (NCEA): https://ncea.acl.g ov/

- FINRA BrokerCheck: https://brokercheck.finra.org/

- ianacare: Look for the ianacare app in your mobile app store, a caregiver locating resource.

- Eldercare Locator: 1-800-677-1116

- Show Me Elder Justice: https://www.elderjusticeformo.org/

ACKNOWLEDGEMENTS

This book exists because I refused to let doubt silence the truth.

When I first discovered the missing jewelry and fraudulent charges, my family didn't believe me. The scope of the betrayal seemed impossible—how could someone we trusted have done this? I spent months gathering evidence, comparing documents, tracing transactions—proving that what looked like paranoia was actually theft.

My attorney was the first person to see what I saw. With over twenty years in probate law, he'd seen cases like this before—but even he admitted ours had elements that were firsts for him. His willingness to take my concerns seriously, even when my own family doubted, gave me the strength to keep going when it would have been easier to let it go.

Fred and his team guided us through the probate process with patience and expertise. He humored my countless theories and scenarios but pushed me forward when I presented evidence that actually mattered to our case. His ability to separate speculation from proof taught me how to build a story grounded in facts rather than anger.

The process of writing proved almost as difficult as uncovering the truth. Nikki gave me the initial encouragement to start this writing adventure when the idea felt overwhelming. Karen Tucker's editorial expertise and Denise McGrail's creative support through the writing process helped me complete the project, providing invaluable guidance on publishing and marketing. Their belief that this story could help others kept me moving forward.

To my family: I know reliving this was too painful for you to participate in the writing, but your support of this project meant everything. We were all hurt by what happened. I chose to channel that hurt into warning others because I believe this group continues to prey on vulnerable people. If this book prevents even one other family from experiencing our loss, it will have been worth it.

To my mother: I'm sorry it took your death for me to see clearly. This book is my promise that your story will open others' eyes before it's too late.

ABOUT THE AUTHOR

Charles E. Wallace Jr. has a technology background in the finance, banking, healthcare, and collections, industries. He is married with two daughters and two grandchildren. When he's not spending time with his family, working or writing, he enjoys coaching youth basketball, outdoor activities, and cooking. *The Caregiver's Game: Unraveling Financial Deceit in the Shadows of Dementia* is his first book.

For media inquires or other information, please contact the author at caregiversgame@gmail.com. You may also visit https://thecaregiversga me.com.

Join My Reader's Group:

https://thecaregiversgame.myflodesk.com/readerslist

www.ingramcontent.com/pod-product-compliance
Lightning Source LLC
Chambersburg PA
CBHW030920120626
46554CB00001B/210

9 7 9 8 9 9 3 3 1 4 4 1 9